PHOTO ODYSSEY

Solomon Carvalho's Remarkable Western Adventure 1853–54

ARLENE B. HIRSCHFELDER

Clarion Books ~ New York

Clarion Books
a Houghton Mifflin Company imprint
215 Park Avenue South, New York, NY 10003
Copyright © 2000 by Arlene B. Hirschfelder

The text was set in 12.5-point Berthold Bodoni Old Face.
Book design by Barbara Powderly.
Map by Barbara Powderly.

Printed in the U.S.A.

Library of Congress Cataloging-in-Publication Data

Hirschfelder, Arlene B.
Photo odyssey : Solomon Carvalho's remarkable western adventure,
1853–54 / by Arlene Hirschfelder.
p.   cm.
Summary: Describes the life of Carvalho, a Jewish photographer
who accompanied John Charles Fremont on his last expedition to the West.
ISBN 0-395-89123-X
1. Carvalho, Solomon Nunes, 1815–1897—Juvenile literature.
2. West (U.S.)—Discovery and exploration—Juvenile literature.
3. Frâmont, John Charles, 1813–1890—Juvenile literature. 4. Photographers—West
(U.S.)—Biography—Juvenile literature. 5. Explorers—West (U.S.)—Biography—Juvenile literature.
6. Jews—West (U.S.)—Biography—Juvenile literature. [1. Carvalho, Solomon Nunes, 1815–1897.
2. Frâmont, John Charles, 1813–1890. 3. Explorers. 4. Photographers. 5. Jews—Biography.
6. West (U.S.)—Discovery and exploration.] I. Title.

F593.C283 H57 2000
917.804'2—dc21

99-042201

CRW 10 9 8 7 6 5 4 3 2 1

To Mickey Pearlman, friend extraordinaire,

who makes fantasies come true,

and Dennis Hirschfelder,

husband and researcher extraordinaire

Contents

Acknowledgments

To Virginia Buckley and Julie Strauss-Gabel at Clarion Books:
your insight and suggestions have made Carvalho shine.

My thanks to:

Anne Dubuisson Anderson for the legal expertise every author needs.

Craig C. Freeman for helping bring Carvalho's prairie grasses to life.

Edith and Max Hirschfelder: for topnotch microfilm research in Alton, Illinois.

Virginia North, archivist extraordinaire, for permitting my husband and me to pour over archival materials about Solomon Nunes Carvalho at the Jewish Museum of Maryland. Jonathan D. Sarna, Joseph H. and Belle R. Braun Professor of American Jewish History at Brandeis University (my alma mater), for guidance in researching American Jewish history. Robert Shlaer for sharing my enthusiasm over an extraordinary photographer's life. Joan Sturhahn for sharing insights about her great-great-grandfather.

Members of Frémont's Fifth Expedition

JOHN BROWN ~ *WYANDOT GUIDE*

CAPERESSIS ~ *DELAWARE GUIDE*

SOLOMON NUNES CARVALHO ~ *DAGUERREOTYPE PHOTOGRAPHER*

JOS COTTER ~ *WYANDOT GUIDE*

NICK COTTER ~ *WYANDOT GUIDE*

FRANK DICKSON ~ *MEXICAN GUIDE*

A. EBERS ~ *PHYSICIAN*

FREDERICK VON EGLOFFSTEIN ~ *MAPMAKER AND TOPOGRAPHER*

JACOB ENIS ~ *DELAWARE GUIDE*

SOLOMON EVERETT ~ *DELAWARE GUIDE*

OLIVER FULLER ~ *ASSISTANT TOPOGRAPHER TO EGLOFFSTEIN*

JAMES HARRISON ~ *DELAWARE GUIDE*

JOHN JOHNNYCAKE ~ *DELAWARE GUIDE*

JOSÉ ~ *RESCUED MEXICAN*

ALBERT LEA ~ *FRÉMONT'S SERVANT AND COOK*

JAMES F. MILLIGAN ~ *GENERAL CAMP HELPER*

JOHN MOSES ~ *DELAWARE GUIDE*

WILLIAM H. PALMER ~ *PASSENGER*

JOHN SMITH ~ *DELAWARE GUIDE*

MAX STROEBEL ~ *ASSISTANT TOPOGRAPHER*

WAHONE ~ *DELAWARE GUIDE*

GEORGE WASHINGTON ~ *DELAWARE GUIDE*

WELUCHAS ~ *DELAWARE GUIDE*

CAPTAIN JAMES WOLFF ~ *DELAWARE GUIDE*

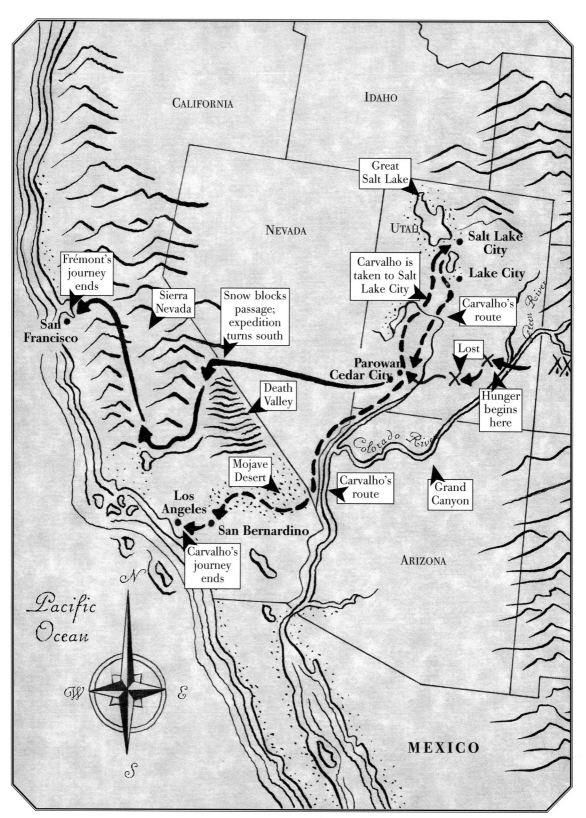

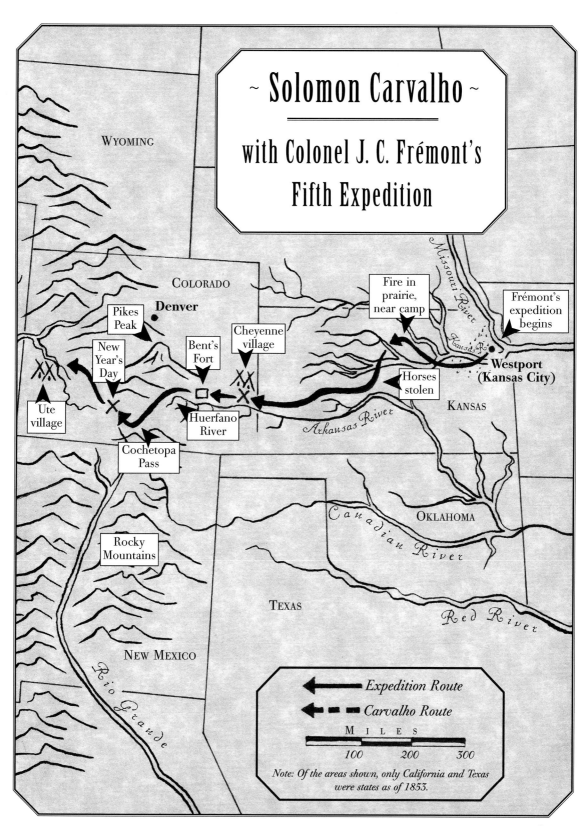

~ Solomon Carvalho ~

with Colonel J. C. Frémont's Fifth Expedition

WYOMING

COLORADO

Denver

Pikes Peak

New Year's Day

Bent's Fort

Cheyenne village

Fire in prairie, near camp

Frémont's expedition begins

Missouri River

Kansas R.

Westport (Kansas City)

Horses stolen

KANSAS

Ute village

Huerfano River

Cochetopa Pass

Arkansas River

Rocky Mountains

Canadian River

OKLAHOMA

TEXAS

Red River

NEW MEXICO

Rio Grande

← *Expedition Route*

←--- *Carvalho Route*

M I L E S

100   200   300

Note: Of the areas shown, only California and Texas were states as of 1853.

Solomon Nunes Carvalho

WHEN THE NOTED EXPLORER AND MILITARY LEADER Colonel John Charles Frémont decided to undertake an expedition in 1853 to explore the best railroad route between the Mississippi River and the Pacific coast, he wanted a photographic record of the journey. He chose an artist and expert daguerreotype photographer from Baltimore, Maryland—Solomon Nunes Carvalho—to accompany him and take pictures.

Carvalho (car-VAH-yoo) was a Jew of Portuguese descent (Sephardic), born in Charleston, South Carolina, on April 27, 1815. As a youngster he witnessed his family's deep involvement in Jewish community life. His father, David, joined a group that tried to reform rituals by shortening services, introducing English into the prayer book, and having the rabbi give the sermon in English. In 1825 David Carvalho helped found the Reformed Society of Israelites in Charleston, the first reform Jewish congregation in the United States. Solomon's uncle Emanuel was a cantor—one who leads chanting of prayers—of a Portuguese congregation in Barbados, and he also served in that capacity in congregations in Charleston and Philadelphia. In 1815, the year of Solomon's birth, Emanuel published the first Hebrew grammar book to be compiled by an American Jew. He was compiling another American Jewish "first," a Hebrew-English dictionary, when he died in 1817.

Like the other members of his family, Solomon Carvalho took pleasure in Jewish community activities. Although little is known about his childhood, his sense of service to the Jewish people, characteristic of his family background, guided him throughout his life. When he lived in Philadelphia in 1849–50, he served as an officer of the Hebrew Education Society. While residing in Charleston in 1851–52, Carvalho joined Shearith Israel Congregation, a traditional

1

John Charles Frémont

The Henry E. Huntington
Library and Art Gallery

Orthodox synagogue. Although he believed Orthodox Judaism should be upheld, Carvalho, like his father, supported important modifications, especially the inclusion of sermons and a portion of the prayers and hymns in English during public worship so Judaism would be comprehensible to those American Jews who did not know the Hebrew language.

Carvalho earned his living through painting, a field in which Jews, especially Orthodox ones, played hardly any role. Early in his life Carvalho showed an interest in art. He traced the beginning of his artistic career to the year 1834, when his family moved to Philadelphia. Undoubtedly he studied the paintings of great painters, spoke with artists in the city, and taught himself how to draw by doing just that— drawing. Within five years of his arrival Carvalho listed himself in the Philadelphia city directories as a portrait painter.

At the age of twenty-three he painted from memory the sunlit interior of Beth Elohim, his childhood synagogue in Charleston. Although traditional Jewish law honored the second commandment, "Thou shalt not make thyself any graven image, nor the likeness of anything that is in heaven above, or on the earth beneath . . . ," Carvalho nevertheless felt he remained true to his traditional Orthodox Jewish beliefs.

When Carvalho was twenty-five years old, he painted *Child with Rabbits*. The painting later was used on paper money issued in the United States and Canada between 1854 and 1864 and as far away as Argentina in 1867. In the United States it appeared on one-, two-, five-, and ten-dollar bank notes. Millions of these bills circulated all over the country, making Carvalho's painting one of the most recognized artworks in North America.

After the introduction of the daguerreotype photograph process in 1839, Carvalho took up that profession as well. Between 1849 and 1853, he opened art and photography studios in Baltimore, Charleston, Philadelphia, and New York. He acquired enough of a reputation to attract the attention of Colonel Frémont.

Child with Rabbits
by Solomon Nunes Carvalho

The Jewish Museum of Maryland

Self-portrait daguerreotype of Solomon Nunes Carvalho

In August 1853 Frémont persuaded the thirty-eight-year-old Carvalho to accompany him as artist and photographer on his fifth expedition to the West. Carvalho, who was at Frémont's side during the five-month journey, kept the only known published record of the entire trip. He chronicled the extraordinary adventures and unspeakable hardships that he, Frémont, and other fellow travelers—ten of them Delaware Indians—experienced on this expedition, which turned out to be the explorer's last.

Carvalho kept his religious practices—apart from some discussions of eating or not eating certain proscribed foods—out of his account. We know far more about his work in the Jewish communities before he left on Frémont's expedition and after he returned to his family. The food that Carvalho was forced to eat on this expedition challenged his beliefs. Traditional Jews observe dietary laws called *kashrut.* Jews keep these laws to honor God. The Old Testament clearly lists which animals were kosher and therefore permissible to eat and which animals were not kosher and thus forbidden to Carvahlo. Animals that have split hoofs and chew their cud are kosher, so Carvalho knew he was limited to grass eaters like cows, sheep, goats, and deer and its cousins. Horses, which are solid-hoofed, and pigs, which have split hoofs but do not chew their cud, were *tref,* or forbidden food for him. But as the expedition progressed into the Rocky Mountains, Carvalho often ate nothing or had to make do with whatever animal, split hoofs or not, the Delaware hunters could kill.

Carvalho also knew that kosher animals must be slaughtered in accordance with Jewish ritual law in order for him to eat their meat. A ritual slaughterer, or *shohet,* severs the animal's jugular vein so it dies instantly and without pain. Kosher slaughtering insures that the maximum amount of blood drains out of an animal's body. Biblical law forbids Jews from eating blood because it contains a creature's essence. After an animal is slaughtered, its flesh must be *kashered* by draining as much blood as possible from the meat and then soaking and salting it to extract any remaining blood before it is cooked.

Any letters Carvalho wrote to his wife, Sarah, that might have shed light on how he practiced other Jewish rituals on the journey have not surfaced to date. Carvalho left no clues as to whether he packed any ritual objects along with his camera equipment. He never mentioned reading a Bible. Nor do we know how he observed the Sabbath over the five months he trekked through the West. We do not know how he observed Rosh Hashanah, the Jewish New Year, or Yom Kippur, the Day of Atonement and the holiest day in the Jewish calendar, both of which occurred while the expedition made its way to Salt Creek.

Chapter 1

A National Mania

I N THE 1840S THOUSANDS OF PIONEERS, mostly white, American born, and from cities on the Atlantic seaboard and villages in the Midwest and upper South, streamed westward. They traveled with their families and relatives and were lured by the tales of incredible riches described in more than thirty guidebooks. Hoping to better themselves, many emigrants headed west over land routes on foot or by horse, wagon, or coach. They hungered for better farms and pastureland and all the fortunes to be obtained from panning for gold. One account told of a miner who had found a gold nugget weighing 839 pounds. Similar stories—plus a tea chest packed with 230 ounces of gold dust and flakes, which was displayed in 1848 at the War Office in Washington—touched off a national mania. After the news in February 1848 that gold had been discovered near what is now Sacramento, California,

> *fifty vessels sailed from American ports for San Francisco. By the middle of March 17,000 persons had taken passage from cities on the Gulf and Atlantic coasts; and before the year closed 230 American vessels reached California harbors. . . . The overland migration, when it began, was even larger than that which came by sea. Within three weeks during the spring of 1849, nearly 18,000 persons crossed the Missouri River for California.*[1]

Not everyone suffered from gold fever. Others went west for religious reasons. In 1846 Brigham Young, the spiritual leader of the Church of Jesus Christ of Latter-Day Saints, read John Charles Frémont's published account of his explorations in 1843 and 1844. Young especially knew about Frémont's writings on Utah. It is said that Frémont's descriptions of the Great Salt Lake area helped the Mormon

7

City folk, gold seekers, and land-hungry families streaming west   Corbis Images

leader make up his mind about a destination for his people. No one else wanted to settle in this place, and here the Mormons could practice their religion in peace.

In February 1848, with the signing of the Treaty of Guadalupe Hidalgo, Mexico ceded the territories of New Mexico and California to the United States. At the end of 1848 the population of California (excluding Native peoples) was estimated at approximately twenty thousand. A year later it approached one hundred thousand. By early 1849 mass meetings of people gathered in several California villages to demand statehood. The movement for direct admission into the Union as a full-fledged state succeeded in 1850, when California became the thirty-first state. Three years afterward, James Gadsden negotiated the purchase of 29,644 square miles of land that would later become part of the states of Arizona and New Mexico.

As the country grew, railroads expanded, too. In 1840 there were three thousand miles of track, mostly in the Northeast, but by 1850 some nine thousand miles of rail connected states east of the Mississippi River.[2] Although no tracks cut through lands west of the Mississippi River, members of Congress believed that construction of a transcontinental railway, stitching together the Pacific coast with the rest of the country, was only a matter of time.

Before the transcontinental railroad was completed in 1869, clipper ships that could accommodate a few passengers sailed from New York to San Francisco via the Isthmus of Panama in the record time of ninety days. But sacks of flour, sugar, and coffee, high boots and saddles, and other trade goods had to be carted west over land on wagons or pack trains, and loaded onto boats and ferried over water. Guns, rifles, and ammunition were sent by this method, too. A railroad stretching from sea to sea would surely solve problems of transportation, shipping supplies, mail delivery, and other kinds of communication. But a big question remained: Where should the tracks be laid? When Congress convened in 1853, a year that saw approximately 27,500 overlanders trail west, almost the entire session was devoted to heated arguments about constructing a railroad to the Pacific. Southern Congressmen did not want a railroad running through northern states, and northern Congressmen did not want a railroad running through southern states. Thomas Hart Benton, the senator from Missouri, insisted that the railroad start in his hometown of St. Louis and cut across the center of the West, at the 38th parallel of latitude. Finally, a suggestion by two senators ended the bitter deadlock. Survey parties could examine possible routes to determine which was the best one from an engineering standpoint. Secretary of War Jefferson Davis, a proslavery southerner in charge of making the appointments, liked the idea. He was confident that the snow-free southern route through Texas would clearly prove to be the best one.[3]

The Thirty-second Congress passed a bill on March 2, 1853, instructing army engineers to survey all of the principal routes and decide which was the "most practical and economical" for a railroad route to the Pacific. Davis sent five surveying parties into the field, each inspecting an important section of the country. However, he did not choose Frémont, a trained mathematician and topographical engineer with considerable experience in the West and an opponent of slavery, to head any of the government-financed surveys.

But nobody stopped Frémont from mounting his own expedition. During his first expedition in 1842, at the age of twenty-nine, he climbed a peak of the Wind River chain of mountains in present-day Wyoming and planted an American flag with thirteen stripes and twenty-six stars in a rock crevice at the summit. On his second expedition in 1843 and 1844, he paddled a rubber boat through the bright green waters of the Great Salt Lake; the spray coated his clothes with a crust of salt. During his third expedition in 1845 and 1846, he fought against Mexico and helped in the conquest of California, and in his fourth expedition in 1848, he battled blizzards in the Colorado Rockies. So Frémont, who was called the Pathfinder by his admirers, now organized his own expedition, financed most probably by Senator

John Charles Frémont in the Wyoming Rockies, 1842

Corbis Images

Benton, who was his father-in-law, and by Frémont himself. Not only did Frémont decide to prove that crossing the snowy Rockies around the 38th parallel of latitude would be the best all-year route for a railroad, but he also decided to cross the region in the middle of winter to test all the difficulties.

As he had on each of his four previous expeditions, Frémont assembled a survey party for this trip to the Rockies. He wanted to be the first explorer to make a photographic record of the trails he blazed. On his first expedition to examine the Oregon Trail from the Mississippi River to Wyoming, Frémont had taken along a camera that produced daguerreotypes, the first real photographs. But he was no good at using the one hundred pounds of daguerreotype cameras, glass plates, cases, and bottles of smelly and sometimes dangerous chemicals needed to develop the pictures on the spot. Charles Preuss, the German mapmaker on that expedition, noted in his diary on August 2, 1842, "Yesterday afternoon and this morning, Frémont set up his daguerreotype to photograph the rocks; he spoiled five plates that way, not a thing was to be seen on them." Five days later, Preuss wrote, "Today he said the air up here is too thin; that is the reason the daguerreotype was a failure. Old boy, you don't understand the thing, that is it." Nine days later, Preuss commented, "Today Frémont again wanted to take pictures. But the same as before, nothing was produced."[4]

As he prepared for his fifth expedition, Frémont once again was determined to have a photographic record, so he purchased a daguerreotype camera. This time he hired Carvalho to make the record.

Chapter 2

Getting Ready

THE DAGUERREOTYPE IMAGE was widely popular in the United States in 1853, even more popular than it was in France, where the process had been invented by Louis Jacques Mandé Daguerre fourteen years earlier. When the inventor died in 1851, the daguerreotype photographers of New York were so upset they wore black armbands on their left sleeves for thirty days.[1]

Frémont may have failed as a photographer, but it took most people only a few days to learn how to take daguerreotypes and required just a small investment of money to start up a business. In fact, approximately two thousand people in the United States were now trying to earn a living with Daguerre's invention, and competition drove prices for a single black-and-white photo down from five dollars to two dollars and fifty cents to one dollar.[2]

Every large city had a number of excellent daguerreotype artists. In 1850 New York City alone had an estimated seventy-seven daguerreotype galleries. And in Baltimore, one of the largest cities in the United States as well as home to the second-largest Jewish community in the country, Solomon Carvalho and eight of his photographic competitors listed their establishments in the city directory.[3] Carvalho's advertisements in the two daily newspapers, the *American Commercial Daily Advertiser* and *The Sun*, also attracted people to his Gallery of Fine Arts. It was located on the second and third floors over Campbell's Jewelry Store at 205 Baltimore Street, in the heart of Baltimore's bustling business district. The famous and not-so-famous wanted their images preserved forever by the magical daguerreotype process. Because Carvalho's newspaper advertisements emphasized that he could take "correct Likenesses of Children" in "two seconds of Time," his studio was also filled from eleven o'clock till three every day with youngsters.

S. N. CARVALHO'S
GALLERY OF FINE ARTS,
NO. 205 BALTIMORE STREET,
(Over Campbell's Jewelry Store,) *Formerly Plumbe's Gallery,*
BALTIMORE.
☞ CRAYON AND MEZZOTINT DAGUERREOTYPES.
Daguerreotypes taken in the *most approved styles,* and warranted not to *rub off.*
Ladies or Gentlemen, having *Pictures* taken at this Establishment, are not required
to pay for them unless they are *perfectly satisfactory.*
The greatest care taken in producing *correct Likenesses of Children,* which, by a new
process, can be accomplished in *two seconds of Time.*
The Gallery is handsomely fitted up; and for the amusement of visitors a *Guitar* and
superior toned *Piano Forte,* from the manufactory of Wise & Brother, has been placed
in the reception room. A private dressing room has been provided for Ladies. Likenesses taken in any weather. Post mortem cases attended to with care and promptness.
Portraits painted in Oil from *Life,* or copied from *Daguerreotypes.* Persons in want
of a classically arranged *Picture,* are politely requested to visit this Gallery.

One of Carvalho's studio advertisements

Ross J. Kelbaugh Collection, The Jewish Museum of Maryland

Carvalho used his reputation as an artist to promote his photography. In his advertisements he boasted that his photographs had an
"artistic arrangement of light and shadow" and resembled "a fine
Crayon Drawing or Mezzotint Engraving." His ads proclaimed that his
daguerreotypes were the best in the city because "they are made by an
experienced Artist who understands the profession scientifically." He
even made colored daguerreotypes, announcing that "experience as an
artist renders him peculiarly qualified." He believed that his gallery
was continually filled with visitors because the rooms were "elegantly
arranged with beautiful specimens of Paintings, Engravings and
Daguerreotypes." While customers waited for their likeness to be
made, Carvalho provided them with a fine-tuned piano so they could
amuse themselves, and there was "a Lady always in attendance for the
comfort of Lady visitors." It is likely these ladies helped women appear
at their very best before the camera's eye.

Filled with the spirit of scientific curiosity, Carvalho mastered the
art of making daguerreotypes, a mirrorlike image of a person or place.
The process involved exposing a highly polished silver plate, usually a
sheet of copper that had been silver-plated and shined to a brilliant

1870s view of Carvalho's original Gallery of Fine Arts at 205 Baltimore Street, to the left of Gallagher's Mercantile College

Ross J. Kelbaugh Collection, The Jewish Museum of Maryland

finish, to iodine vapors in a wooden camera until the silver surface turned a bright golden yellow. The image on the exposed plate was then treated to mercury fumes heated by flame. After the silver plate was washed in water and dried, it was fitted like a jewel into a specially manufactured velvet-lined brass case that was sometimes as small as a child's hand or as large as twelve by fifteen inches. Since no negative or proof was left behind to use again, each framed daguerreotype image was one of a kind and could never be reproduced. The image made from the exposed plate was crystal clear, with no hint of glare. No portrait painter, not even one as accomplished as Carvalho, could compete with the amount of detail the mirrorlike daguerreotype provided. There was one big problem, however. Everything used in processing the image—mercury fumes, iodine gas, and other chemical solutions—was poisonous. Some daguerreotypers even died from breathing air charged with these fumes!

Fortunately for the photographers, the process of making daguerreotypes came to an end when the photographic process headed in another direction, in which negatives were produced. From these negatives any number of positive prints could be made—the leading principle of all modern photography.

On August 22, 1853, while Colonel Frémont was in New York City purchasing scientific equipment for his expedition, he sent for Carvalho. Although the two men had never met, each knew of the other's reputation. Frémont had probably seen one of Carvalho's ads in the newspapers and city directories of Philadelphia, Baltimore, or Charleston listing him as a professional daguerreotypist. Or perhaps he was aware that Carvalho had invented a protective enamel cover for daguerreotypes to replace the breakable piece of glass placed over the image.

Like most Americans at the time, Carvalho knew about Frémont's

Interior of a daguerreotype studio, 1853

previous explorations of the West and admired him as a hero, states-man, and man of adventure and courage. During a brief meeting between the two men, the explorer invited the daguerrian to accom-pany him as the official photographer of his expedition. Although Carvalho had never been west of the Mississippi River and had not the remotest idea about the life-threatening dangers and bone-chilling cold involved in exploring mountainous regions during winter, he accepted without thinking twice. He did not even ask his wife, Sarah, for her opinion. Nor did he think about missing his young sons, David and Jacob, and daughter, Charity. This was a dream come true for a man who hungered for the excitement of new places and adventures and who probably wanted a break from years of posing fidgety chil-dren and fashionably dressed city folk. This trip would give him an opportunity to use his considerable knowledge of the daguerreotype process during an adventurous journey and to make a contribution to the new and growing country he loved. Carvalho's profound respect for Frémont increased when the citizens of Charleston, Solomon's birthplace and the city where Frémont had spent his youth, honored the colonel's achievements with a sword and golden scabbard.

In the journal he wrote several years after the expedition, Carvalho recalled his reaction to Frémont's invitation:

> *A half hour previously, if anybody had suggested to me the probability of my undertaking an overland journey to California, even over the emigrant route, I should have replied there were no inducements suffi-ciently powerful to have tempted me. Yet, in this instance, I impulsively, without even a consultation with my family, passed my word to join an exploring party, under command of Col. Fremont, over a hitherto untrodden country, in an elevated region, with the full expectation of being exposed to all the inclemencies of an arctic winter.*[4]

This was not Carvalho's first adventure. When he was about nine-teen and a salesman in the West Indies traveling on his uncle's mer-chant ship, the boat was wrecked during a storm. Carvalho swam to shore towing the other passengers and crew members to safety with a rope. He experienced a second shipwreck in 1845 during his honeymoon in the West Indies. Solomon took Sarah, his new bride, on a cruise in the islands, and the ship on which they were returning was destroyed. Neither event deterred Carvalho from further travel and adventure.

Before Carvalho was scheduled to join Colonel Frémont in St. Louis, he had two weeks to acquire the equipment he needed. He spent ten days making preparations for the journey. Experience had taught him how to develop daguerreotypes in warm studios, but making them on mountaintops in temperatures plummeting to thirty degrees below zero would require special equipment. He arranged for the proprietor of a major photo supply house in New York City to make up new fuming boxes, chemicals, and other instruments. In addition to his camera apparatus, Carvalho packed painting materials and also took along half a dozen cases of preserved coffee, eggs, cocoa, cream, and milk supplied by a Mr. Alden. Before 1853 canned food was a rarity in the United States. Alden wanted Carvalho to test the preserved food under difficult travel and weather conditions to see whether the ingredients stayed perfectly preserved and maintained their nutritious qualities. Carvalho calculated that the tins of preserved food had "sufficient nourishment to have sustained twenty men for a month."

After leaving New York on September 5, 1853, Carvalho arrived at the Illinois River, where he planned to cross over to St. Louis. The river was so low that steamboats were inoperable, so he was advised to take a stagecoach to Alton, Illinois, a prosperous Mississippi River town and busy crossing point to St. Louis. But Carvalho was bogged down with heavy cases of photographic instruments, and the owner of the stagecoach refused to take them on board. Carvalho, already way behind schedule, told the stagecoach owner how disappointed Colonel Frémont would be if he and his equipment did not get to St. Louis on time. Fortunately for Carvalho, the mere mention of the colonel's name changed the coach proprietor's mind. He had accompanied Frémont on one of his previous expeditions and was convinced, he told Carvalho, that "a nobler specimen of mankind does not live in

TRANSPORTATION.

INCREASED SPEED—REDUCED RATES.
THE CHICAGO AND MISSISSIPPI RAIL-
ROAD, after March 1st, will transport freight at the
following reduced rates, without any extra charges:
FIRST CLASS—From St. Louis to Springfield.... 32cts
SECOND do —..........."..............24cts
The deduction of twenty-five per cent.
heretofore made on certain articles, in
lots of 15,000 pounds, will be made hereafter on these arti-
cles, in lots of 10,000 pounds.
On and after 1st March, Freight trains will leave Alton at
12 M.; by which arrangement freight will be delivered at
Springfield in 24 hours from St. Louis.
For further information apply at the C. & M. R. R. wharf
boat, St. Louis, or the Freight offices at Alton and Springfield.   [m6d&wtf]   E. KEATING, Sup't.

JACKSONVILLE AND CARROLLTON R.
ROAD.—Notice is hereby given, that the undersigned, having been appointed for that purpose, will,
on the 18th day of October, at the office of Geo. T. Brown,
in the city of Alton, open books of subscription of the capi-
tal stock of said company.   GEO. T. BROWN,
oct3 tf   E. KEATING,   Com'.
                                     LEVI DAVIS,

ALTON, AND ST. LOUIS PACKETS.—The
splendid steamers Altona, Capt. W. P. La-
mothe, and Cornelia, Capt. D. C. Adams, make
daily trips, (Sundays excepted,) between the
cities of St. Louis and Alton, connecting, at the latter place,
with the Railroad to Springfield.
HOURS OF DEPARTURE.
Altona leaves Alton at.........................9 A. M.
"   "   St. Louis at........................6 P. M.
Cornelia leaves St. Louis at,..................9 A. M.
"   "   Alton at...........................1 P. M.
Passengers will be careful to be on board at the above
hours.   oct15 tf

RITCHERDSON'S
DAILY ALTON AND ST. LOUIS EXPRESS.
On and after Monday, February 28th,
the above EXPRESS will leave Alton every
morning by the Altona, and return every evening, under the
immediate charge of J. F. RITCHERDSON. All business in-
trusted to his care, will be strictly attended to. Packages,
Parcels, Orders, and money conveyed and delivered prompt-
ly. Notes, Accounts, Drafts, &c. collected and paid. Pur-
chases made, and a general Express and Commission busines-
transacted.
PACKAGES TO SPRINGFIELD.
THIS EXPRESS will transmit all packages to
Springfield and intermediate points on the
Railroad, daily. Light freight put through by this Line from
St. Louis, 24 hours in advance of the usual way.
                                JOSEPH F. RITCHERDSON.
Office at Capt. Post's store, Piasa street, late "Smith
Pickard," and on the boat.

STEAM FERRY AT ALTON,
THE undersigned hereby informs the public
that his new steam Ferry-boat is now
completed and in fine running order. Teams
and stock will be ferried across, from Alton to
points on the Missouri shore of the Mississippi river, with
speed and at short notice.
TO EMIGRANTS.—Alton is on a line with St. Charles and St.
Joseph, Mo., and excellent roads; therefore, emigrants for
California and Oregon will do well to cross at this point.—
The MARION has plenty of machinery and steam, and will
run ten miles per hour up stream, with perfect safety. All
pains taken to accommodate. Towing of flatboats, barges,
wood carrying, and all other jobs of that sort, performed
with dispatch, and on the most reasonable terms.
Remember the New Steam Ferry.
m31   THOMAS BROWN

STEAM FERRY AT ALTON,
THE undersigned hereby informs the public
that his new steam Ferry-boat is now
completed and in fine running order. Teams
and stock will be ferried across, from Alton to
points on the Missouri shore of the Mississippi river, with
speed and at short notice.
TO EMIGRANTS.—Alton is on a line with St. Charles and St.
Joseph, Mo., and excellent roads; therefore, emigrants for
California and Oregon will do well to cross at this point.—
The MARION has plenty of machinery and steam, and will
run ten miles per hour up stream, with perfect safety. All
pains taken to accommodate. Towing of flatboats, barges,
wood carrying, and all other jobs of that sort, performed
with dispatch, and on the most reasonable terms.
Remember the New Steam Ferry.
m31   THOMAS BROWN

*Advertisement for ferry-boat service across the
Mississippi River from the* Alton Telegraph,
September 2, 1853

Author's collection

these parts." An extra team of horses was immediately harnessed, and
Carvalho's heavy boxes were stowed on board. Carvalho was not even
charged for his passage or for the freight of the boxes, which together
would have amounted to eight dollars, a lot of money in those days.

Carvalho ferried across the Mississippi River by steamer to St.

St. Louis, Missouri, 1853

Missouri Historical Society

Louis and arrived just in time on the doorstep of the mansion where Frémont was staying. That same afternoon, September 8, Frémont and Carvalho left by steamer for Kansas City. On board were other people hired for the expedition: a German baron named Frederick von Egloffstein, who, along with his partner, a Mr. Zwanziger, advertised themselves in St. Louis newspapers as "surveyors and topographical engineers," and Oliver Fuller, an assistant to Egloffstein, also from St. Louis, who was chosen to go along because he had made a previous crossing to California, mostly on foot. To play it safe, at the last minute Frémont had also hired another photographer, a German-born Mr. Bomar, because Frémont thought Carvalho was not going to arrive on time—if at all.

Chapter 3

A Camera, a Contest, and Camp Life

FTER LANDING AT KANSAS CITY on September 14, wagons transported Colonel Frémont, the other members of the expedition, and the baggage to a campsite near Westport (now part of modern Kansas City), a starting point for expeditions heading west. Carvalho and Bomar found comfortable lodgings at a hotel, where they busied themselves going over their equipment. Bomar planned to take pictures by a competing method of photography, one that produced wax-paper negatives from which multiple prints could be made. He spent several days preparing the paper. Carvalho doubted whether photographs could be made quickly enough by that process when unexpected storms, wild animals, or other dangers would surely threaten them. Frémont decided to hold a contest between the two men. The one who most quickly developed a picture of a scene from the window of his hotel room would become the expedition's official photographer.

Solomon Carvalho disappeared behind a black wooden box and covered his head with a black drape. After inserting into the camera a silvered plate buffed to perfection, he removed the lens cap, exposed the plate for several seconds, then replaced the cap to stop the exposure. He then exposed the daguerreotype plate to the vapors of heated iodine and bromine in the fuming box, and held the plate over fumes of heated mercury. He fixed the image with a preservative to make it permanent. In the space of thirty minutes from the time Frémont gave the word, Carvalho's daguerreotype was ready. But Bomar's photograph could not be seen until the next day. According to James F. Milligan, who served eleven weeks with the expedition, Bomar did not have a portable darkroom and was forced to wait until nightfall to develop his photograph.

Since Colonel Frémont could not provide a portable darkroom,

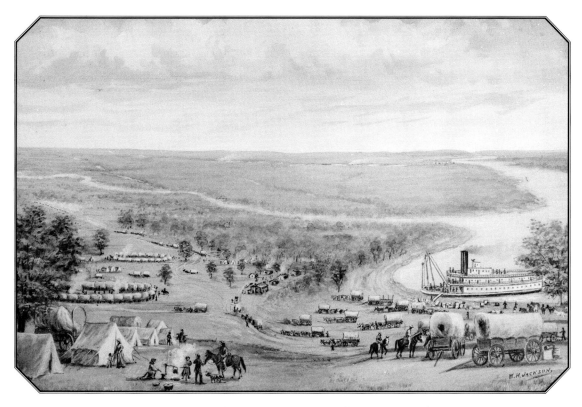

Westport Landing, *a painting by William Henry Jackson*

he let Bomar go and chose Carvalho as the expedition's sole photographer. But just in case Carvalho was finding too burdensome the responsibility of having the expedition's photographic record depend entirely on him, Frémont offered him the opportunity to back out. He even offered to pay him for his time.

Of course Carvalho knew that he would not be able to work in the field as fast as he had in his hotel room, where the daguerreotype apparatus could be neatly laid out. In the open country it usually took two hours to make one daguerreotype view. Most of that time was spent in unloading the camera, fuming box, and plates and in preparing the chemicals and washing the plates. Then all of it had to be reloaded into the baskets used to carry the equipment.

The muleteers, who cared for the mules that carried the equipment, had to pack and repack the apparatus each time the equipment was needed. Before the expedition had barely inched its way west-

Daguerreotype outfit, 1847

ward, the muleteers already resented Carvalho for the delays and the extra work. As far as the packers were concerned, Carvalho's heavy baggage was their biggest nuisance. When his carrying baskets were destroyed around the end of September, Carvalho believed that the packers had "accidentally" done it on purpose.

Carvalho decided to replace the baskets with even stronger carrying cases. He found some covers and sides from old dry-goods boxes and carried the load by horseback to the home of a blacksmith some ten miles from the group's campsite near a Potawatomi village. The proprietor was not home, but his wife gave Carvalho the run of the workshop. Spying a saw and hatchet, he went to work and made the apparatus boxes himself. When he returned to camp with the replacements, the muleteers were astonished and all "their bright hopes that the apparatus would have to be left were suddenly dissipated."[1]

Throughout the journey Carvalho watched the muleteers closely.

Twice he found the tin case that held his buffer in the road. It had slipped off the mules "from careless packing—done purposely." Without this one instrument Carvalho would not have been able to make his daguerreotypes.

When Carvalho accepted Frémont's offer to join the expedition, he had no idea what living under the open sky truly meant. In Baltimore he posed people for pictures on the third floor of his studio under a glass ceiling that permitted natural lighting; there, he and the subject were completely shielded from rain or snowstorms.

On his first night in camp Carvalho got a taste of life in the great outdoors. The rains came, and each sleeping man—as well as his clothes and bedding—was soaked. Carvalho was assigned the job of purchasing waterproof coverings to protect all of the explorers from more stormy weather. The next day he managed to purchase two dozen India-rubber blankets from an outfitter in Independence, Missouri. Made from the milk of a tropical rubber tree, the smooth black waterproof blankets were now the single most useful article

Mules were well-suited for long trips.   Corbis Images

NEW YORK INDIA RUBBER WARE HOUSE, No. 27 Malden Lane and 59 Nassau street.—Factory foot of Twenty-fifth street, East River.—The undersigned manufacturer and dealer in every variety of India Rubber Fabrics, would call the attention of merchants and others in pursuit of Rubber Goods to the extensive assortment to be found at the above establishment, amongst which are the following— 400 pieces of 3-4, 4-4 and 5-4 plain and figured India Rubber Carriage Cloths, made of heavy drills and good gum.

Coats,	Life Preservers,	Air Beds,
Cloaks,	Air Beds	Knee Caps
Capes	Air Pillows	Suspenders
Sou' Westers	Air Cushions	Boots
Leggins	Carriage Cloths	Bottles
Overalls	Machine Belting	Tobacco Wallet
Pantaloons	Steam Packing	Tents
Gloves	Hospital Sheeting	Horse Fenders
Mittins	Travelling Bags	Horse Covers
Armlets	Navy Bags	Canteens
Maps	Camp Blankets	Haversacks
Bath Matts	Croton Hose	Gold Bottles
Artists' Gum	Mining Boots	Cups
Money Belts	Wading Boots	Shoulder Braces
Gun Covers	Baptismal Pants	Suspenders
Nursing Aprons	Bathing Caps	Elastics, &c. &c.

Also patent metallic and perpetual gloss over shoes of every variety, Providence and City mills do heavy, for country trade, common or Para rubbers, furred and lined do. &c. &c.

The above are of the most approved manufacture, are warranted and are offered for sale on liberal terms, at very low prices, by   D. HODGMAN,
       New York India Rubber Warehouse,
       No. 27 Malden lane, and 59 Nassau street

d19

1850 New York Post advertisement for India-rubber (waterproof) merchandise

Author's collection

owned by the men. They cared for these ugly black blankets as if they were fine handmade bed linen. Carvalho wrote in his journal that the explorers

placed the India-rubber blanket on the snow, our buffalo robes on top of that for a bed, and covered with our blankets, with an India-rubber blanket over the whole—India-rubber side up, to turn the rain. We generally slept double, which added to our comfort, as we communicated warmth to each other, and had the advantage of two sets of coverings. During the whole journey, exposed to the most furious snow-storms, I never slept cold, although when I have been called for guard I often found some difficulty in rising from the weight of snow resting on me.[2]

Another hardship presented itself when Carvalho, a man accustomed to sitting on chairs upholstered with damask, selected his mount, a pony named Pongo that was trained to hunt buffalo. Carvalho, who had never ridden a horse before, explained:

> *This animal was given into my own charge, and I only then began to realize that I had entered into duties which I was unqualified to perform. I had never saddled a horse myself. My sedentary employment in a city, never having required me to do such offices; and now I was to become my own ostler [hostler], and ride him to water twice a day, besides running after him on the prairie for an hour sometimes before I could catch him.*[3]

But within a day Carvalho could saddle his pony like an experienced cowboy. And on September 24 he saddled Pongo at dawn and rode for a considerable distance from camp. He stood in complete

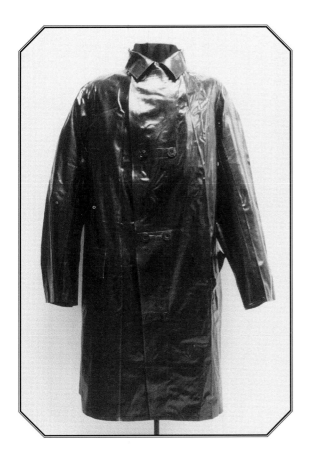

India-rubber raincoat, c. 1865

DeSoto National Wildlife Refuge,
U.S. Fish and Wildlife Service

silence in the midst of an immense, swaying sea of grass glittering in the morning dew and watched the sun rise. Overwhelmed by the sublime scene before him, Carvalho stared at the eastern horizon as it

> *assumed a warmer hue, while some floating clouds along its edge, developed their form against the luminous heavens. The dark grey morning tints were superseded by hues of the most brilliant and gorgeous colors, which . . . softened, as the glorious orb of day commenced his diurnal course, and illumined the vault above . . .*[4]

He stood in the midst of inconceivable beauty, but there was no one to share it with, and Carvalho suddenly longed for his other life and the comforts of home. Although he questioned whether he should continue on this journey, he decided, "I will onward, and trust to the Great Spirit, who lives in every tree and lonely flower, for my safe arrival at the dwelling of my fellowmen, far beyond the invisible mountains over which my path now lies."[5]

As the weather got colder, the requirements of camp life became harder to fulfill. For example, each man in the camp was expected to bring in a certain quantity of firewood. When it was Carvalho's turn, he realized that he did not know how to chop wood. He didn't even have the physical strength to use the ax correctly. So he hunted through the woods and managed to find several decayed tree limbs, which he hauled back to camp on his shoulder. After three trips, he had gathered just enough kindling wood for one night. Carvalho believed in doing as much work as the others and did not expect to warm himself at their expense, but he quickly understood that searching for firewood was "not a very congenial occupation."

Each man in camp was also expected to take care of his own dirty laundry. Solomon gathered together three weeks' worth of worn shirts, stockings, handkerchiefs, and underwear and asked one of the muleteers to wash them. To his surprise, not even a lowly muleteer wanted to earn money in that way. Solomon had to become his own "washerwoman." He got some soap, gathered up his duds, and went to the bank of a creek, where, for the first time in his life, he washed his own clothes and hung them out to dry. But not before he rubbed the skin off his hands during this operation. Carvalho figured that laying the items carefully under his bedding while he slept would take out the wrinkles. The next morning he discovered that his clothes were as smooth and flat as pancakes.

Chapter 4

Buffalo Hunting

HORTLY AFTER THE EXPEDITION set forth from Westport, Colonel Frémont began to suffer from sciatica, a burning pain that traveled down his legs. He returned to St. Louis for medical treatment and asked his fellow explorers to travel to a rendezvous point near Uniontown, situated in present-day western Shawnee County, Kansas, on the south bank of the Kansas River. Here they would make camp with a group of Delaware Indians until his return.

The Delaware ancestral lands had been taken from them, and by the 1850s they had been pushed westward into Kansas Territory. But they were still famous as skilled hunters and guides, and some tracked beaver all the way to the Rocky Mountains. In fact, Frémont had hired some of the best Delaware men as guides and hunters for his third expedition. On his fifth expedition Frémont again decided to hire Delaware, paying each man two dollars a day to accompany the expedition and supply the group with buffalo, venison, and other game. The Delaware had to use their own animals, but Frémont agreed to supply them with ammunition. Most of these Delaware spoke English, and they all understood it. Solomon Everett, who had accompanied Frémont on his third expedition, told Carvalho that he "would have ventured his life" for Frémont. That was because the colonel never asked his men to do anything he himself wasn't willing to do. He treated and respected all men as equals, and they, in turn, respected him.

Colonel Frémont notified the men by letter that while he was getting medical treatment they should move their encampment to the Saline Fork of the Kansas River. Plenty of buffalo could be found there, and the location at Salt Creek (now called the Saline River) was ideal for an extended stay. Clearly impressed, Carvalho wrote descriptions of the country that would have pleased a trained biologist:

Chief James Sagundai,
Delaware guide,
accompanied Frémont
on his third expedition.

The Bancroft Library

There are numerous streams of water in the Territory. . . . The country is well watered, and on all the rivers grows timber of large size and in great variety. The river bottoms are very fertile, being covered with an alluvial black soil from twelve to twenty-four inches deep. . . . Another bottom over which the waters must have once flowed is elevated about sixteen feet from the river, and high up some sixty to seventy feet, lies the immense undulating prairie, teeming with buffalo, blacktail deer, antelope, sage and prairie chickens. . . . The second bottoms are studded with groves of timber. The various kinds of oak, maple, elm, red-flowered maple, black walnut, locust, beech, box, elder, wild-cherry, and cotton-wood attain a large size, and are to be found on the Kansas River and its many tributaries in quantities.[1]

Kansas, he said, had "grasses of a hundred different kinds," some of them tall enough to hide a six-foot man. These grasses grew spontaneously on the prairies and nourished immense numbers of game. The only thing that spoiled this otherwise perfect location was the Kansas River. Because the water was the "color of the character of the soil over which it passes," it was not fit for making daguerreotypes. To finish his plates, Carvalho had to wait until he reached the "crystal streams from the Rocky Mountains."

During the first week, the Delaware hunters brought several kinds of game into the camp. Oliver Fuller, the group's most successful hunter, shot wild turkeys, ducks, and a rabbit. Even Carvalho became expert at hunting game after he spent some time shooting at targets. He noted, "At one hundred paces, I have hit the 'bull's eye' twice in five times, which is not bad shooting, considering I have had no practice since I was a member of a rifle volunteer company in Charleston, some twenty years ago."[2]

Hunting was so successful that James F. Milligan, a general

Prairie grasses   Jim Brandenburg, Minden Pictures

Wild turkeys   U.S. Fish and Wildlife Service

helper, said the camp looked like "a Game Depot on a large scale, having everything in the game line from a teal duck to a Buffalo."[3] The men had so many choices that their biggest problem was deciding which animal to eat.

During the four weeks of waiting for Colonel Frémont's return, the men broke the monotony by hunting, gunning, and preparing buffalo and antelope meat in different ways. Carvalho even got accustomed to eating buffalo hump rib soups. Some of the men challenged one another to target practice and bet pancakes on the outcome of the contest. Others started to think about the hard times to come and busied themselves by cutting and drying meat. They would soon be heading into the Rocky Mountains, and there meat would be scarce. Some nights, while the men were asleep, wolves roamed near their camp and ravaged portions of the dried meat, stealing chunks of it from the drying racks and running off into the woods.

Carvalho watched the men feasting on huge portions of heavily salted game and drinking sugared coffee and tea three or four times a day. He was worried that "we shall want some of the good things which are now being inconsiderately wasted." He was right. Salt and sugar quickly ran out, and by October 20 the camp was entirely out of flour. John Johnnycake, one of the Delaware guides, and William H. Palmer, a "passenger" on the expedition who was chosen by Frémont to supervise the encampment, had to go back to Fort Riley, Kansas, fifty miles northeast of the camp, for more provisions.

At daylight on October 25, the Delaware Weluchas, "a most successful hunter, and as brave and daring an Indian as ever fashioned a moccasin or fired a rifle," approached Carvalho and asked him if he wanted to go on the hunt. He had been tempted to go before, but this invitation clinched it. He grabbed his rifle, revolver, and sheath knife and rode out of camp with eight Delaware and four other white men. The buffalo that had been sighted near their camp at Salt Creek three weeks earlier had now moved about fifteen to twenty miles south, an unfailing sign to mountain men that a hard winter was on its way. After a three-hour ride, the group reached the brow of a hill. Carvalho beheld, with astonishment and delight, a spectacle he would never have seen on the crowded city streets of Baltimore. Below him was a large herd of six thousand buffalo—bulls, cows, and calves. The animals, which were grazing on abundant and nutritious short-curled "buffalo" grass, covered the floor of an extensive valley. Carvalho wrote:

> *It was a sight well worth travelling a thousand miles to see. Some were grazing, others playfully gamboling, while the largest number were quietly reclining or sleeping on their verdant carpet, little dreaming of the danger which surrounded them, or of the murderous visitors who were about to disturb their sweet repose.*[4]

The men stood silently, waiting to see in which direction the herd would move when it sensed the presence of the hunters. An old bull was stationed several hundred yards in advance of the herd, and he warned the herd. Suddenly, as if by magic, the whole herd was in motion. They moved fast, like racehorses. But they could still be killed

Buffalo   Kansas State Historical Society

quickly by a hunter if he hit them in a relatively small area behind and below the left shoulder. The animals were at a disadvantage because instead of standing their ground and fighting like grizzly bears or scattering like antelopes, they tended to consolidate the herd and flee in a straight line.

At a signal from the Delaware, the whole party, except for Carvalho, galloped after the herd. Captain James Wolff (one of the Delaware), Weluchas, and the others rode their horses near the buffalo. Resting their rifles on their saddles, they each kept one leg in a stirrup for balance and threw the other leg over the rifle to steady it. Leaning to the side until their eyes were level with the animal, they took a quick sight, then fired. Even riding at full speed they rarely missed the mark.

Transfixed by the sight, Carvalho almost forgot why he was there. For a while he ignored his pony, who was chomping at the bit. His animal, too, wanted to chase buffalo. Finally, Carvalho spied what he thought was a fat buffalo cow and rushed after it at full speed. After

Hunting buffalo   The Henry E. Huntington Library and Art Gallery

chasing it for two miles, he stopped, took sight with his rifle, fired, and wounded the buffalo cow in the leg. He reloaded, started again at full speed, fired once more, but missed. He took out his pistol, and when he got within range discovered he had chased an old bull instead of a cow. Bulls, he knew, were tough and hard and were usually hunted by Indians for their hides, not their flesh. Even though a typical bull weighed over a ton, it could run at speeds of thirty-five miles an hour.

Now Carvalho fired his pistol four times at the bull and was trying to keep him in sight when the bull suddenly spun around and came within fifteen feet of Carvalho's pony. The animal instantly jumped aside, as it had been trained to do by the Indian who once owned it. The bull stopped, its huge body thrown off balance by its wounded leg. Taking advantage of the moment, Carvalho fired his rifle, this time mortally wounding the beast. As the buffalo lay dying, Carvalho approached it and later wrote that it "turned his large black eyes mournfully upon me, as if upbraiding me with having wantonly and uselessly shot him down."

After recovering from his fright and excitement, Carvalho discovered that not one human being or buffalo was in sight. He was alone in the middle of a valley carpeted with short, curly buffalo grass. Unlike his Delaware companions, who seldom chased an animal farther than a mile, Carvalho had mistakenly ridden at least five miles away from the other men. Without a pocket compass he did not know what direction to take back to camp. He rode to the top of a nearby hill and spied Smoky Hills, a geographical landmark twenty miles in the distance. Fortunately for Carvalho, after riding about an hour, whom should he find but Weluchas, dismounted and walking slowly, eyes fixed on the ground, looking for a tomahawk pipe he had dropped while hunting.

The two men rejoined the hunting party, where Captain Wolff and another Delaware were cutting up a fine fat cow. Carvalho tried to help but gave up after attempting to remove the liver. Years of painting human anatomy had not prepared him to butcher buffalo. On the way back to camp Carvalho told the men about his adventure with the old bull, finishing his story by stating proudly that he had killed this huge animal. But Captain Wolff corrected him. According to tradition, Captain Wolff explained, Carvalho had not really killed the buffalo,

Supplying Camp with Buffalo, *a painting by A. J. Miller*

because he had not cut out and brought home the animal's tongue. In his journal Carvalho wrote:

> *Gentle reader, do you think I was equal to cutting out, by the roots, a tongue from the head of an old buffalo bull, after telling you that I did not succeed in getting out the liver of a young cow, after the animal was opened? Surely I was not; but even if I had been, the alarming situation I found myself in, at the time he fell, prevented me from attempting it, if I had known it was the hunters' rule to do so.*[5]

Chapter 5

Prairie Fires and a Cheyenne Village

SETTLERS AND EMIGRANTS dreaded prairie fire season in the fall, a time when everything they owned might go up in flames. At the end of October 1853 the prairies were on fire, and they burned for several days. The members of Frémont's party watched as a "most disagreeable and suffocating smoke filled the atmosphere." It rose higher and higher, forming a dark cloud that blocked the sun like an eclipse. During the night, Carvalho saw the dark cloud assume a "horrible, lurid glare all along the horizon. As far as the eye could see, a belt of fire was visible."

Still, the men felt relatively secure from danger. The prairie was bordered by the Kansas River on one side, the Smoky Hill River on the other, Salt Creek on the third, and a large belt of woods about four miles from camp on the fourth side. The Delaware tethered all the animals near the creek and stored the baggage near the water for safety. But when Carvalho took his guard post at two in the morning, the whole horizon seemed to be ablaze. By dawn he saw that the forest, a shelter for mules and horses only hours before, had been reduced to ashes and the smoky, blackened remains of tree trunks.

Carvalho had lived in several cities, and he knew that spectacular blazes could wipe out whole blocks and on windy nights threaten an entire city. He did not know that setting prairie fires was an ancient and valuable tool and that Indians regularly set fires to kill off trees and shrubs that would spread over the prairie grasses and turn the open land to forests. They set the fires to lure game animals to the new grass that sprouted within days after a fire. These grasses also nourished their horses. When natural forces like lightning ignited grasses and forests, flames cleaned out thickened mats of dead grass that choked off the smaller grasses and wildflowers and fertilized the soil. It made traveling during summer and fall easier, since old grasses would not entangle the feet of either horses or men.

Escaping a prairie fire   Kansas State Historical Society

    The fires were growing, but Frémont's men still did not want to budge because he had instructed them to stay put until he returned. Solomon Everett had gone back to St. Louis to guide Frémont to the camp. The men were afraid Solomon would find it difficult, if not impossible, to locate the group if it moved to another location.

    On October 31 time was running out. Suddenly one of the Delaware pointed to an open space beyond the campsite. There, to the great joy of the men, was Colonel Frémont, galloping through the blazing grass in the direction of the camp. He was followed by Everett and by Albert Lea, Colonel Frémont's cook. With them was a huge man named A. Ebers, who was perched on a large feather bed that was saddled to an enormous mule. Ebers, a German-born doctor who listed himself in the St. Louis business directory as a homeopathic physician, had been hired by Frémont to accompany the expedition. The four men had ridden through forty miles of country that had been, or still was, on fire. The trail that led to the camp had been obliterated. Nevertheless, Everett had accurately directed them back to the spot where he had left the group. Now the men in the camp fired their rifles into the air to signal to the four approaching riders. They reloaded, and when the four came closer, they fired a welcoming salute.

Once Colonel Frémont and the others reached the camp, his men packed the animals so that they would be ready to depart at daylight. While they packed, winds kept the fires back, but toward night the winds changed direction. The fire crossed the river. The camp was surrounded by smoke and flame on every side. No outlet appeared. The only escape was for the men to ride their horses at full speed through one hundred feet of blazing grass. As Frémont gave the orders, all the men dashed into the fire, with the colonel himself leading the charge. Men and horses all emerged unscathed and untouched. Within minutes the danger was over, and for the rest of the day the group traveled over a burned, blackened, smoking prairie.

Colonel Frémont galloping into camp

From *Incidents of Travel and Adventure in the Far West,* copyright 1954 by the Jewish Publication Society

During the first week of November, as the group traveled westward, the prairie between Walnut Creek and the Arkansas River was covered with short buffalo grass. The herds of buffalo were so large that the prairie looked black. Perhaps, thought Carvalho, there were at least two hundred thousand animals. At one point the men were forced to stop for more than an hour while a single herd galloped at full speed across their path. Carvalho wanted to take daguerreotypes of the buffalo in motion, so George Washington, one of the Delaware guides, ran an old bull out of the herd to about thirty feet from Carvalho's camera. That was too close for comfort or picture-taking, and the photographer made a wild dash to safety. Although he never succeeded in photographing moving animals, he did make several pictures of distant herds.

The group camped on the open prairie, where the thermometer registered temperatures well below the freezing point. No firewood or

Buffalo on the move   Jim Brandenburg, Minden Pictures

timber could be found to build a warming fire, so two of the men went looking for fuel. They returned carrying a blanket filled with buffalo chips. Buffalo grazing on prairie lands left behind dung, or "chips." These priceless chips were one of the explorers' most important sources of fuel when there were no trees to cut down. A fire built with buffalo dung stayed hot for a long time without giving off much smoke or odor. Carvalho said:

> But for this material, it would be impossible to travel over certain parts of this immense country. It served us very often, not only for cooking purposes but also to warm our half frozen limbs. I have seen chips of a large size—one I had the curiosity to measure was two feet in diameter.[1]

Gathering buffalo chips

Kansas State Historical Society

While Frémont's men were camping on the prairie, the man guarding the horses made a big mistake. He left his post after midnight without arranging for anyone to take his place, and while he was warming his frozen hands and feet before a large fire, three mules and two ponies were stolen. The Delaware discovered moccasin prints in the snow and determined "from their peculiar form" that they had been made by Cheyenne. But the fresh horse tracks had been made by shod horses, so the Delaware knew immediately that these were the stolen ponies. Indians, they knew, did not shoe their own horses.

It took several days to reach the Cheyenne village, which was situated along the Arkansas River in a spot called Big Timber, a twenty-mile stretch of cottonwood forest. There they found Frémont's animals mixed in with other fine horses, some of which had been raised by the Cheyenne. Most, according to Carvalho, were "stolen and taken as prizes in their forays with other tribes of Indians." Some of the Cheyenne acknowledged that they had watched Frémont's camp during the night, waiting for an opportunity to steal the animals. When the guard left his watch, they quickly made off with five of them. The thieves even "went so far as to point out the very man who went to the fire."

The Cheyenne village at Big Timber contained one thousand men, women, and children who lived in more than two hundred fifty lodges. Carvalho entered the village to make some daguerreotypes, but it was not easy to get the images he wanted. Sitting still in front of a

Big Timber along the Arkansas River   The Henry E. Huntington Library and Art Gallery

Cheyenne lodges Western History Collections, University of Oklahoma Libraries

small black box on stilts was a new experience for these Cheyenne people. At first Carvalho had trouble convincing anyone to sit for a portrait, so he took pictures of their lodges and one of an old woman and a baby. After the people saw the actual images, he had no problems taking pictures of a younger woman and several of the chiefs. "They thought I was a 'supernatural being,' and, before I left camp, they were satisfied I was more than human," he wrote.[2]

Carvalho also dined with the chief of the village. He noticed that the chief's lodge, while larger than the others, did not differ in other respects. While he ate buffalo steaks and venison, Carvalho studied the lodge's interior. He saw that the only furniture consisted of beds made from cedar branches covered with buffalo robes, on which the chief's two wives and three children slept. Under the beds were their moccasins and neatly folded deerskin shirts. The women, he learned, prepared the animal skins and made everyone's clothes and moccasins. They also built the lodges and arranged the furnishings inside. They selected the village sites and erected and took down the lodges every time the Cheyenne moved their villages—usually three or four times a

Daguerreotype of Cheyenne village by Solomon Nunes Carvalho   Library of Congress

year. The men hunted with bows and arrows (also made by the women), fished, and fought. At that time—in the autumn of 1853—they were at war with the Pawnee.

Carvalho saw that the women loved ornaments. Most wore bracelets made of thick brass wire, but a few possessed silver bangles "beaten out as thin as pasteboard." The beautiful daughter of the head chief wore brass bracelets and fine robes decorated with elk teeth, beads, and colored porcupine quills. After Carvalho took her picture, he motioned to her to hand him one of her brass bracelets. Reluctantly, she gave him one. He wiped it clean and "touched it with 'quicksilver' [mercury]. Instantly, it became bright and glittering as polished silver." The young woman was astonished to see her bracelet suddenly transformed. She "slipped it over her arm, and danced about in ecstasy."[3]

Within an hour everyone in the village knew about Carvalho's ability to "convert" brass into silver. He was surrounded by women begging him to make their brass bracelets and rings shine. But he needed the remaining quicksilver to make his daguerreotypes and had to refuse nearly all the moccasins and venison offered as payment. He was so popular that he even had to turn down an invitation to remain and live with the Cheyenne.

It was just as well that Carvalho needed to conserve the mercury. This shiny, silver-colored liquid poisons the central nervous system

*Old Cheyenne
woman and baby*

The Bancroft Library

Cheyenne woman erecting a lodge   Kansas State Historical Society

and causes tremors, memory loss, headaches, and vision and speech problems. The Cheyenne were better off without it.

Carvalho returned to camp with many pictures and about a dozen pairs of new moccasins, some elaborately worked with beads. He packed them away in his boxes and from time to time, when his companions most required and least expected it, he gave away a pair.

Chapter 6

Supplies for the Journey

T HE EXPEDITION NEEDED SUPPLIES, so Frémont led the group to Bent's log trading houses in the Big Timber area of the Arkansas River known as "the mountains" or "the Upper Arkansas." (In 1862 the region became part of Colorado Territory.)

William Bent had been employed by his older brother, Charles, in the firm of Bent, St. Vrain & Company, which managed the company's Indian trading center at Bent's Fort in Colorado. After his brother was killed in an Indian uprising at Taos in New Mexico Territory in 1847, he dissolved his partnership with Ceran St. Vrain in 1848 and became the sole owner of Bent's Fort.

For more than fifteen years, from its construction in 1833, Bent's Fort was the dominant structure in the entire Southwest, a trade empire that covered parts of nine present-day states and in the 1840s was the largest Indian trading fort between St. Louis and the Pacific Ocean. Hundreds of miles from any settlement, it stood near the hunting grounds of the Cheyenne, Arapaho, Comanche, Ute, and Kiowa Indians. Shoshone, Crow, and Gros Ventre from the northern plains visited the fort as well.

William Bent was married to Owl Woman, and, after her death, to her sister, Yellow Woman, daughters of White Thunder, an important Cheyenne chief. Bent was a shrewd trader. He wanted to control the Indian trade in the area. When the tribes camped nearby, he invited them into the fort. The Indians performed dances, and he arranged feasts and gave out presents of paints, knives, looking glasses, and handkerchiefs. Bent's Fort became a popular campsite for the Indians.

Every spring Bent took twenty-five to thirty wagons and a herd of horses, mules, and cattle from the fort, which was on the north side of the Arkansas River, to Westport, Missouri, on the Missouri River, a distance of some five hundred miles. The wagons carried all the buf-

Big Timber area of Arkansas River   The Henry E. Huntington Library and Art Gallery

falo hides and furs and silver bullion that had been acquired from Indians and trappers during the fall and winter. On return trips to the fort, Bent carried soap, candles, tarpaulins, vinegar, hard bread, beans, rice, cloth, and other goods to trade to Indians and emigrants. In that great stretch of plains between the fort and the Missouri River, there was not a single house, ranch, stage line, settlement, trading post, or government fort of any kind.

In 1849 Bent tried to find a buyer for Bent's Fort. Some accounts say that when the federal government offered an outrageously low price for the fort, Bent partially destroyed it in disgust and then abandoned it rather than accept the offer. Other accounts say he burned the fort to stop a cholera epidemic. The army later acquired Bent's Fort and in 1862 renamed it Fort Lyon.[1]

Bent had already moved his wagons and men in 1849 to a better site for his trading business—on the north bank of the Arkansas River below Big Timber. Here the Cheyenne, Arapaho, Kiowa, Comanche, and Prairie Apache often camped, about thirty-eight miles downstream from the old fort and a mile upstream from the site of the new fort.

The new fort was under construction when Frémont's expedition arrived in the area in November 1853.

Big Timber had an abundance of oak and cottonwood and large quantities of stone for building. The site was also directly in the path of emigrants and travelers who needed supplies as they made their way to Santa Fe. Carvalho wrote:

> *Bent's House is built of adobes, or unburnt brick, one story high, in the form of a hollow square, with a courtyard in the centre. One side is appropriated as his sleeping apartments, the front as a store-house, while the others are occupied by the different persons in his employ. . . . Bent's House is a trading post. Indians of the different tribes bring in their venison, buffalo meat, skins, and robes, which are exchanged for various descriptions of manufactured goods.[2]*

Colonel Frémont and his men camped near Bent's new fort for about a week. The time was spent in "refitting and preparing proper

William Bent

Colorado Historical Society

Bent's new fort

camp equipage for the journey over the mountains." Frémont obtained fresh horses and mules for all the men, a small buffalo-skin lodge for himself, and another large enough to hold twenty-five men. Bent had only a small quantity of sugar and coffee but supplied Frémont with all he could spare. The colonel also acquired considerable quantities of dried meat and moccasins, overshoes, and buffalo robes for each man, as well as stockings and gloves.

Since Frémont was now healthy, he decided not to take Dr. Ebers over the mountains and made arrangements with Bent to send him back to St. Louis on the first wagon train. Carvalho regretted that Dr. Ebers was staying behind because the two men had ridden side by side for many miles, and the doctor had entertained the photographer with his knowledge of botany and geology. Carvalho asked the doctor to take his tin case of paints and brushes back home, since he had found the weather too cold for painting. Frémont also asked James F. Milligan, who disapproved of the explorer's domineering style of leadership, to stay behind at the fort and care for the worn-out animals until the colonel returned from his expedition. Since Milligan's feet were blistered from heel to toe and so painful that he could not stand on them, he was glad to stay at the fort. When Milligan bid the expedition good-bye on November 25, the group consisted of twenty-one men and fifty-four shod animals.

After the expedition broke camp, Colonel Frémont led the group along the banks of the Arkansas River until it reached the mouth of the Huerfano River. The men followed that river to the Huerfano Valley, "the most romantic and beautiful country" Carvalho had ever beheld. Across the Huerfano River stood a granite rock formation called Huerfano Butte, or the Orphan, which rose straight up more than four hundred feet from the flat valley floor. Colonel Frémont wanted a daguerreotype of this spectacular-looking butte even though he knew it would take one to two hours for Carvalho to make a single image. Most of that time was needed to repack the equipment into boxes and reload the mules. Luckily Egloffstein, Fuller, and two of the Delaware remained with Carvalho to help him distribute the heavy boxes evenly on the mules.

The five men knew they were now four hours, or twelve miles, behind the main party. They followed the group's trail through the immense fields of artemisia until nightfall covered the tracks of Frémont's men. They tried to signal the main camp with rifle fire, but

Lower mouth of Huerfano Canyon   Colorado Historical Society

high winds carried off any return signal and it was impossible to determine where or how far away the camp was located.

They had no other choice but to stay put for the night and build
a large fire to keep warm; the weather was "intensely cold and disagreeable." When they unpacked the animals, they discovered baggage
and buffalo robes for all the men but not one thing to eat or drink.
And even though they wanted to curl up in those warm robes and go
to sleep, they stayed awake and watched over their mules so they
would not stray. In the main camp the men also stayed awake. They
were gathered around the fire, trying to keep warm. Without the
warmth of their buffalo robes, they could not sleep.

Carvalho's group would not have had to go hungry had he been
ready to divulge his secret store of tin boxes filled with preserved eggs

Hunting Bear, *a painting by A. J. Miller*   Walters Art Gallery

and milk. But it was better to go hungry one night, he thought, and to save the special food for a "more pressing occasion."

At dawn the hungry men packed the animals and found the lost trail, and soon they encountered some of the very men whom Frémont had sent to find them. And when they reached camp, they found a breakfast of buffalo and venison waiting. Nothing could have tasted more delicious.

More was soon to be added to the menu of buffalo and venison. The Delaware hunters had spotted fresh bear tracks, and the two men who first spied the enormous black bear chased after it immediately. The bear saw the hunters approaching at full speed and tried to escape, but the first bullet brought the animal to its knees, and three shots killed it. The bear provided several days of much-needed food for the whole party, but when Carvalho tried to eat a small piece, he found it "too luscious and greasy for [his] palate." The traditional Jew from Baltimore had not yet been transformed into a bear eater.

Chapter 7

Rocky Mountain Summits

THE EXPEDITION NOW FACED the Rocky Mountains—sheer, insurmountable walls with sharp, jagged peaks. Actually, as they moved westward, the expedition had to get over three lofty mountain ranges—the Wet, the Sangre de Cristo, and the San Juan. Like immense fences, the sawtoothed mountain rims prevented many emigrants from reaching the Pacific Ocean, unless they knew where to find the high mountain passes and the valleys in between.

These notches provided a practical way for people to get through a forbidding mountain wall. Some passes were barely distinguishable, but others reminded explorers of the miraculous parting of the Red Sea. The awesome mountains seemed to draw back so that people and animals could pass. The map division of the United States Geological Survey counts more than three hundred named passes in the Colorado mountains where this phenomenon occurs, more than one hundred of them in the southern Rockies.

Colonel Frémont led his expedition over the Wet Mountains and through the Sandhill Pass (now called Medano Pass) in the Sangre de Cristo range, one of the oldest passes in the southern part of Colorado. Then he and Carvalho briefly left the party and inspected the Roubidoux Pass (now called Mosca Pass), ten miles below Sandhill. The mostly red peaks at sunset give these mountains their Spanish name, which means "the Blood of Christ." From the summit of the Roubidoux Pass, the photographer got his first view of the San Luis Valley and the headwaters of the Rio Grande. Carvalho made a daguerreotype of the distant valley and the San Juan Mountains stretching across forty miles. While the two men were exploring the pass, they stumbled on a Mexican named José who was barely clothed and could hardly walk. He had been deserted by some hunters. In one of many humanitarian moments, Colonel Frémont was moved to take the man back to camp. He gave him clothes from his own wardrobe and permitted him to join the expedition.

Frémont's group descended into the San Luis Valley by way of the Sandhill Pass. In the valley they chose a campsite and raised their tents. They were scarcely settled when a herd of black-tailed deer came down a mountain to drink from a nearby stream. That night, thanks to the Delaware hunters, the men suppered on "fine roast venison." Frémont decided to remain at the camp for several days so that his hunters could kill deer and cure the meat for the trek through the mountains. He knew that game would soon be impossible to find.

The journey continued into the Cochetopa Mountains. Colonel Frémont led the ascent up the mountains through trackless, sparsely timbered forests to the summit, which was covered by a forest and about four inches of snow. Surrounding the group were immense granite-gray mountains whose peaks were covered with snow. A trail for a wagon road had been cut through the dense forest of tall trees that grew at the summit. Fortunately for Frémont, he had found the trail made a few months earlier by Captain John W. Gunnison, who had led one of the government-sponsored survey teams to find a railroad route to the Pacific. Trees felled to clear the path for Gunnison's wagons marked the way, even with snow on the ground.

On December 14, 1853, the men noted that the streams that had been running toward them now ran in the opposite direction, and they knew they had crossed the Continental Divide. This ridge runs along the summit of mountains several miles above sea level through what is now west central Colorado. The barrier divides the waters of the continent, which flow away from it in opposite directions, with drainage in the west running into the Pacific and drainage in the east ending up in the Atlantic Ocean. Reaching the Continental Divide gave the expedition "gratifying proof that we had completed our travel to the summit, and were now descending the mountains towards the Pacific." The group left the woods and camped on the edge of a rivulet.

Near the camp a rugged mountain, barren of trees and thickly covered with snow, interested both Frémont and Carvalho. Both knew that a daguerreotype from its summit would reveal the surrounding

Cochetopa Pass

countryside for hundreds of miles, but its approach was inaccessible by even the most surefooted mules. The way up was steep, around rocky walls, with stones of all sizes from pebbles to boulders weighing tons embedded in the soil, and small ledges of rock croppings at various points. Despite the danger, Carvalho asked Frémont to have two men help carry his camera equipment so he could climb the mountain on foot and make pictures from its summit. Since Carvalho was determined to go, and knowing that one misstep could mean Carvalho's life, Frémont accompanied him. It took three hours to reach the top, but the difficult struggle paid off. They

> *beheld a panorama of unspeakable sublimity spread out before [them]; continuous chains of mountains reared their snowy peaks far away in the distance, while the Grand River plunging along in awful sublimity through its rocky bed was seen for the first time. Above us the*

cerulean heaven, without a single cloud to mar its beauty, was sublime in its calmness. Standing as it were in this vestibule of God's holy Temple, I forgot I was of this mundane sphere. . . . I looked from nature, up to nature's God, more chastened and purified than I ever felt before.[1]

They were standing in Cochetopa Pass, meaning "buffalo gate" in the Ute Indian language. Because buffalo could cross through it at almost any season of the year, the Spanish and Mexicans called it El Puerto de los Cíbolos, or Port of the Buffalo. As Lieutenant Edward G. Beckwith noted later in his survey report, "No mountain pass ever opened more favorably for a railroad than this." Nestled in the San Juan Mountains at an elevation of 10,149 feet, Cochetopa Pass offered a gently sloping, easy route across the Continental Divide.[2]

Plunged up to his waist in snow in Cochetopa Pass, Carvalho made a panorama of the continuous ranges of mountains around them. While the pictures were being processed, Colonel Frémont made "barometrical and thermometrical observations" and examined the rocks. After the work was completed, they descended, hungrily eating their dried buffalo and deer meat.

Chapter 8

Horses and a Surprise Save the Day

SOLOMON THANKED "the great Omnipotent" for his survival in thirty-degree-below-zero weather. He felt that God had saved him, but he also knew that all those weeks of eating, sleeping, and traveling in the open air had toughened his body and prepared his muscles and bones for the intense cold of late December in the Rocky Mountains.

Snow covered the immense mountain over which the expedition had to travel. Each man followed in the hoof prints of the horse and rider before him until all the members of the group were together at the foot of the mountain. There they dismounted and led their animals along an "intricate and tortuous path." As usual, Carvalho brought up the rear, following his unbridled and riderless pony. The snow was so deep that when he fell, he was literally up to his neck. And on this particular day Carvalho had to pull himself out of a snow-filled chasm. His pony, however, was not in the mood to wait, and Carvalho saw it gallop after the rest of the party—about one hundred fifty feet ahead. Exhausted and unable to pursue the animal, Carvalho sank down on a rock. He was alone, on foot, and "on the mountains of eternal snow, with a long day's journey before [him]." And he was afraid, his heart pounding so fiercely that he could count each beat. From the top of a nearby hill he saw the trail of the expedition in the frozen snow. As he followed the tracks of the men down the mountain, he slipped, sometimes falling ten to fifteen feet. But a miracle awaited him at the bottom of the mountain. There was his pony tied to a tree. Captain Wolff had caught the riderless animal and tied it up in a place where Carvalho was sure to find it. Carvalho felt as though he had been delivered from certain death. He was probably correct.

On New Year's Day 1854 there were many reasons to celebrate. Everyone was alive. Carvalho brought out his two secret tin boxes,

An uphill struggle

which he had cared for as if they were sacred objects. Inside were hermetically sealed egg yolks beaten to a thick paste, plus a pound of sugar and dried milk preserved with powdered sugar. Carvalho also had in his trunk a supply of powdered arrowroot, which his wife had packed in case he had bowel troubles. But arrowroot is also a valuable food, useful for making milk puddings. With these ingredients and six gallons of boiled snow water, Carvalho whipped up a blancmange, or white milk pudding, a favorite dessert of French aristocrats as far back as the fourteenth century. After making "as fine a blanc mange as ever was *mangéd* on Mount Blanc [a mountain in the French Alps]," he kept his treat secret from Colonel Frémont and the other men.

After a dinner of horse steaks, Carvalho served up his surprise:

The satisfaction and astonishment of the whole party cannot be portrayed, when I introduced, as dessert, my incomparable blanc mange. Six gallons of bona fide, nourishing food, sweetened and flavored! It is hardly necessary to say that it disappeared in double quick time. The whole camp had a share of it; and we were all sorry that there was no more left of the same sort.[1]

This was the men's last "feast" on the expedition. Soon after New Year's Day, food ran dangerously low, and the men were forced to eat rations of meat biscuit, a far cry from blancmange. This was prepared by saturating flour with the juices of boiled beef and then baking the concoction into a biscuit. But it would hardly keep the men alive for long, and soon they had to kill their horses to survive. Pongo, Carvalho's buffalo hunter, now broken down, was one of the first to be sacrificed. The animal that had so bravely carried him on his first buffalo hunt was unable to bear even a bundle of blankets. The horse meat gave the men the energy to trudge on.

Several days after coming down from Cochetopa Pass, the group reached the Grand River (now called the Gunnison). They began to climb a high, steep mountain of snow, but halfway up a terrible accident occurred as the party tried to avoid a chasm of the river. One of the baggage mules lost its balance. Its hind legs had sunk deep in the

Snow-covered mountain peaks   James Blank, Bruce Coleman, Inc.

snow. Down it tumbled, pulling the other animals with it, all rolling headlong down the snowy mountain and unable to stop themselves from falling several hundred feet to the bottom. It was amazing that only one mule and one horse were killed. Bales of buffalo robes and blankets were scattered everywhere. Even the tent poles that supported the large lodge were smashed when they hit the trees. But Carvalho's boxes of daguerreotype equipment landed uninjured, cushioned by and buried in the snow.

The party needed food. While the camp settled down in a cozy place near a creek fringed with willows and cottonwood, the Delaware men rode out and killed a fat young horse. While they were out hunting, they also discovered fresh footprints of Ute Indians. The Ute lived in a village in the Uncompahgre Valley nearly twenty miles away. They had been renowned for trading in horses ever since acquiring them in peaceful exchanges with the Spanish around 1630. Colonel Frémont was looking for fresh mounts and wanted to trade with the Indians for desperately needed supplies. But he also knew that around 1846 the Ute had set fire to Fort Uncompahgre, which sat at the confluence of the Grand and Uncompahgre Rivers. (Since the 1820s, the Ute homeland had been invaded by British and American explorers, trappers, traders, and white settlers, including more and more Mormons.) Frémont doubled the guard and examined each man's Colt revolver and rifle to make sure they were in working order. Carvalho suspected that his double-barreled gun might not shoot. He had used his rifle as

Ute Village   The Henry E. Huntington Library and Art Gallery

a walking stick to help him descend the mountain and to dig himself out of snowdrifts. Indeed, when he tried to fire it, the gun did not go off. The barrels were filled with frozen snow. Carvalho received a stern lecture from Frémont about the uselessness of a gun that did not fire.

To trade with the Ute, Colonel Frémont moved the camp closer to their village. It contained many lodges, housing several hundred people. The Indians received the expedition "very kindly." The men traded some blankets, knives, red cloth, and other wares for fresh horses and venison.

Hours after the trading, while the men were eating deer meat, they heard loud noises approaching the camp. When Carvalho checked to see what was causing the commotion, he found what appeared to be the entire Indian community—men, women, and children—assembled around the lodge. Carvalho and one of the Ute men who spoke Spanish acted as interpreters. The Ute told Carvalho that the horse the Delaware hunters had killed the day before belonged to one of the women. She valued it very highly and insisted that Frémont's men had no right to kill it without paying her for it. At first the Indians turned down Frémont's offer of reimbursement for the horse and demanded a share of everything in the camp, including a keg of gunpowder. After Frémont refused, it looked as though the Indians might attack. The colonel suspected that the Ute would not risk a fight, because the women and children were present. After considerable talking, the Ute people accepted Frémont's earlier offer.

One of the Ute men returned with a beautiful three-year-old dark bay colt full of "life and fire." He offered to trade it to Carvalho. Tired of walking or hitching rides on a baggage mule, Carvalho was permitted to trade for the horse "one pair of blankets, an old dress coat, a spoiled daguerreotype plate, a knife, half an ounce of vermilion [for face and body paint], and an old exhausted pony, which we would have been obliged to leave behind."

Glad to be riding a horse again, Carvalho departed with the party. The peppy horse, who winced a little under the first bit it had ever had in its mouth, cantered obediently. Suddenly, about two miles out of camp, Carvalho discovered that he had carelessly left his revolver behind. Frémont sent him and Frank Dickson, a Mexican, back to the deserted camp to look for it. When the pony found its head turned toward home, it chomped at the bit, got it between its teeth, and took off with the speed of a bullet. Carvalho wrote:

> *In less than five minutes I found myself in a wild sage bush on the road; the saddle had slipped round his body, which was smooth as a cylinder, while I, losing my balance, slipped off. My pony was quietly grazing in the Indian camp, when I, riding double with Frank, arrived there. The most important thing was my pistol; I proceeded immediately to the spot, and, hidden in the long grass, where I laid it down, I found it.*[2]

The Ute captured Carvalho's pony and resaddled it. Mounted once again on the frisky pony, Carvalho left the Ute village, and he and Dickson overtook the party after a two-hour ride.

The pony bucked and kicked Carvalho, especially when he tried

Packed horse

Corbis Images

to saddle it. One morning as he was saddling the pony, the animal reared and came down with both feet on Carvalho's chest. Frémont came to his rescue. He asked Albert Lea, the cook, who was accustomed to breaking in horses, to exchange horses with Carvalho until the photographer's horse had calmed down. Carvalho gladly accepted the offer and rode out of camp on a cream-colored pacer "much lighter in spirits." But his good mood did not last long, for the cook's horse was so lame that on the second day Carvalho could no longer ride it. On foot again, he watched the cook ride by on his beautiful pony, wishing he had been brought up as an "ostler and professional horse-breaker."

The expedition followed the Uncompahgre River until it reached the Grand and then followed it to the Colorado River. But they still had to travel six hundred feet across the Grand to the opposite shore. And this crossing was going to make the dash through the prairie fire look like child's play. First the men scattered sand on the eighteen-inch-thick ice that bordered their side of the river so that the animals wouldn't slip on the frozen surface. Even so, they could barely keep their footing. The river was six feet deep, so the animals would have to swim to the other side. And they definitely did not want to leap from the ice into the roaring waters. Colonel Frémont was the first to force his horse into the punishing current, inspiring his men to follow. Once they were in the freezing water, only the heads of the animals and men bobbed above the surface. Carvalho understood that

> *To arrive at a given point . . . it was necessary to swim your horse in a different direction to allow for the powerful current. I think I must have been in the water at least a quarter of an hour. The awful plunge from the ice into the water, I never shall have the ambition to try again; the weight of my body on the horse naturally made him go under head and all; I held on as fast as a cabin boy to a main-stay in a gale of wind. If I had lost my balance it is most probable I should have been drowned. I was nearly drowned as it was, and my clothes froze stiff upon me when I came out of it.*[3]

Mountain Torrent, *a painting by A. J. Miller*   Walters Art Gallery

Despite the ice and freezing current, the whole party crossed the river safely. Some of the Delaware, many of whom made it to the other side before the white men, built a large fire, at which the soaking but grateful men dried their clothes.

Chapter 9

To Eat or Not to Eat

AFTER THE DANGEROUS RIVER CROSSING during the last week in January, Colonel Frémont gathered the men together for an urgent meeting. These men had already eaten mule and bear to survive. But Frémont wanted to make sure that what had happened on his fourth expedition would not be repeated. On that trip, he had been trapped by blizzards in the Rocky Mountains and had sent four men to the nearest settlement for help. One died, and Frémont recorded in his memoirs that the other three ate part of the man's body for food. More likely, historians say, animals or vultures ate the dead man, but Frémont felt that the three survivors were guilty. He now told his men that cannibalism revolted him. He wanted them to promise that none of them would, under *any* circumstances, kill anyone else in the party. He threatened to shoot the first man who even hinted at such an idea.

Frémont never mentioned the ill-fated Donner party. He didn't have to. The story of the grisly 1846 incident in the Sierra Nevada in California was widely known. Reports of the catastrophe reached New York City by July 1847. Most people, including Frémont's party, knew that eighty-seven emigrants and teamsters headed for California had been trapped in the Sierras by one of the stormiest winters in memory. The newspaper accounts reported that blizzards, twelve-foot snowdrifts, sub-zero weather, and starvation forced some of the gaunt and frostbitten survivors to eat several of their dead comrades for food. The sheer will to live made people resort to cannibalism. But the men on this journey swore to avoid it.

Carvalho was deeply moved by their pledge.

It was a solemn and impressive sight to see a body of white men, Indians and Mexicans, on a snowy mountain, at night, some with bare head and clasped hand entering into this solemn compact. I never until

Colonel Frémont pledging members of the expedition against cannabalism

From *Incidents of Travel and Adventure in the Far West,* copyright 1954 by the Jewish Publication Society

that moment realized the awful situation in which I, one of the actors in this scene, was placed.[1]

The men went to sleep without supper on beds of snow, with no prospect of anything to eat in the morning to energize them for another day's trek. But Carvalho still had faith that they would survive, and he remembered the verses of Psalm 107 and felt assured he would be delivered from hunger and thirst:

> *They wandered in the wilderness in a solitary way: They found no city to dwell in. Hungry and thirsty their souls fainted within them. Then they cried unto the Lord in their trouble, and he delivered them out of their distresses. And he led them forth by the right way that they might go to a city of habitation.*[2]

When it was necessary to slaughter their horses and mules for food, Carvalho wrestled with himself over whether or not to eat them. Clearly they were not allowable meats according to Jewish law. To make matters worse, they had not been slaughtered by a *shohet*, and their meat was not kashered. Usually Carvalho was able to refrain from eating mules and horses, but when exhaustion drained him of strength, he changed his mind, in accordance with *pikuach nefesh*, the Jewish belief that the importance of preserving life takes precedence over almost all other Talmudic laws. He ate these strange and forbidden foods with hesitation and only in small quantities.

> *The taste of young fat horse is sweet and nutty, and could scarcely be distinguished from young beef, while that of the animal after it is almost starved to death is without any flavor; you know you are eating flesh, but it contains no juices—it serves to sustain life, it contains but little nutritive matter, and one grows poor and emaciated, while living on it alone. Mule meat can hardly be distinguished from horse meat, I never could tell the difference.*[3]

After one twenty-four-hour period without food, a Delaware hunter killed a coyote. It was divided equally among the men. Carvalho left his portion untouched, preferring to fast another twenty-

Coyote eat dead flesh

U.S. Fish and Wildlife Service

four hours rather than eat coyote. Carvalho explained, "The habits of the horse and mule are clean; their food consists of grass and grain; but I was satisfied that my body could receive no benefit from eating the flesh of an animal that lived on carrion."[4]

For thousands of years Jewish dietary laws had emphasized cleanliness. Since coyotes ate dead and putrefying flesh, Carvalho assumed their meat was unfit for consumption and that his stomach would reject it. As if to prove his point, the men who ate coyote meat were seized with cramps and fits of vomiting.

Beaver—food for hungry men

U.S. Fish and Wildlife Service

On the night of the pledge against cannibalism, Oliver Fuller, who was on guard duty, spotted a beaver swimming across the stream. He lifted his rifle to his shoulder, fired, and killed it so the men could eat breakfast. But he forgot that discharging a rifle during the night watch was a signal that Indians were approaching. Carvalho had seen wolves come into the camp on the Saline Fork of the Kansas River. They stole buffalo meat, yet the Delaware never allowed a gun to be discharged. The sudden shot of a rifle made a tremendous explosion, the sound reverberating along the rocks and echoing in the valley of the river. Instantly, the whole camp was awake. Colonel Frémont rushed out of his lodge, guns in hand. The other men, too, were ready to fight.

Instead, they were greeted by one of the Delaware dragging after him an immense beaver, the animal that Fuller had killed. Since everyone was so hungry, Colonel Frémont, who usually punished any man who broke a rule, never said a word to Fuller. The sight of something to eat instead of something to fight had changed his mood.

Carvalho ate large, furry rodents, but he drew the line at rodents covered with stiff, sharp quills on their back. When the Delaware hunters arrived in camp one day with a thirty-pound porcupine, they first burned off its quills, leaving a thick, hard skin, "like that of a hog." Since kosher dietary laws especially emphasize prohibitions against eating pig, Carvalho's stomach revolted at the sight of the white, fatty meat that looked to him like pork. He chose to go hungry while the others enjoyed their meal.

Soon afterward, Frémont's party traveled southwest, following the course of a dry stream to the Green River, past the western limits of what is now the state of Colorado, and into Utah. Again, the men had not tasted food for nearly two days, and they were exhausted from hunger. Their spirits lifted when they spotted several Indians on the opposite shore, who welcomed them to their village. The people living there were nourished by grass seed that tasted like roasted peanuts after the women parched and ground it between stones. They gathered the seed in the fall, but this was late January and there was little

Carvalho drew the line at eating porcupine.

U.S. Fish and Wildlife Service

left in the village. The party could only acquire a small supply. Carvalho traded everything he could part with from his daguerreotype boxes, plus several articles of clothing for a quart of seed. That supply lasted for three days, and he found it nourishing and easy to digest. Indeed, he felt he had regained his physical energy because of the "sustaining properties of this cereal."

Chapter 10

Stubborn as a Mule

MORE TROUBLE STARTED at the end of January. Even rubber blankets could not protect the group from what Carvalho called "the heaviest and most drenching rain-storm" he would experience on the five-month journey. The expedition was now camped in the entrance of a valley that looked like a primeval forest. Their feet sank deep into layers of dead leaves that had fallen from the limbs of huge trees. Although there was no snow, the weather was cold and raw. The men made up their beds, as usual placing their India-rubber blankets first on the decayed leaves. Carvalho retired early, exhausted from "traveling over a rugged country of volcanic formation, with an apology for moccasins on my lacerated and painful feet." He slept until midnight, when he was awakened by cold water running between his clothes and body. When he uncovered his head, he realized that it was raining hard and steadily. Within an hour the water was nearly a foot deep. His blankets and robes were saturated, and his wet clothes clung to his skin. At dawn the men discovered that all their equipment was soaked except for the daguerreotype apparatus. Carvalho's time-consuming packing had protected the cameras from the rain.

Then the muleteers started to pack the mules carelessly, and bales of blankets and buffalo robes slipped off the animals' backs as the men were descending from a steep mountain. Mules were obedient if they were bridled and packed correctly. But when one got free from its load, the animal asserted itself and took off at full speed. Then it took an hour for the men to recapture and repack it.

Carvalho discovered that when a mule was determined not to budge, only a man with extraordinary patience could get it going again. Because Carvalho was often in the rear—since he stopped to make daguerreotypes—he assisted the muleteers in driving up the animals that lingered on the road. The muleteers and mules were always at the end of the parade.

Carvalho learned quickly about a mule's obstinate behavior. The animal assigned to him after his horse was killed always needed to eat and was busy searching for grass or wild bushes under the deep snows. Carvalho tried to grab the mule's thirty-foot-long lariat, which was trailing along the ground, and the moment he thought he had it, the mule dashed away at a full gallop, pulling Carvalho through the snow. When he let go of the lariat, his hands were lacerated and almost frozen. But he tried again. He gently approached the mule, gathered the rope in his hand, patted it for a few minutes, and then jumped on its bare back.

The life and activity he possessed a few moments before is entirely gone; he stands like a mule in the snow, determined not to budge a step. I coax, I kick him. I use the other end of the rope over his head; he dodges

Mules—stubborn but dependable   Kenneth W. Fink, Bruce Coleman, Inc.

the blow; but his fore-feet are immovably planted in the snow, as if they grew there. I, worn out, and almost frozen, remain chewing the cud of bitter reflection, until one of my comrades comes to seek and assist me; he goes behind the mule and gives him a slight touch à posteriori [in the hindquarters]; when, awakening from his trance, he starts at a hard trot into camp, quietly submits to be saddled, and looks as pleasantly at me as if he were inquiring how I liked the exercise of catching him. Similar scenes occurred daily . . . "Stubborn as a mule," is an o'er true adage, as I can fully testify.[1]

One day the group trudged fifteen miles over a snow-covered range. When they looked around, the mule that was carrying the bales of red cloth and blankets to be traded with Indians was not to be found. None of the muleteers remembered seeing it during the day. Two men retraced the path made by Frémont's party to look for this special animal, considered to be the most well-trained and docile of all the mules. Eventually the men found it standing behind a tree in exactly the same place where it had been packed. When the other animals were driven out of camp that morning, it had been overlooked. It had not moved a muscle for at least twelve hours.

Mexican mules—the type of breed the men had—were noted for their endurance and ability to travel long distances and did not require as much feed as horses. They operated on what would have been starvation rations for a horse. Despite their stubbornness, Carvalho appreciated the dependability of Mexican mules and valued them for it. He noted that

a mule will thrive on provender [dry food for livestock] that would starve a horse. If a mule gives out from exhaustion; with a day's rest, and a good meal, he will start on his journey, and appear as fresh as he ever was; but if a horse once stops and gives up, it is over with him, he is never fit for travel again.[2]

Chapter 11

Frozen Feet and Dead Animals

EGLOFFSTEIN AND HIS ASSISTANT, Fuller, generally brought up the rear of the train with Carvalho because mapping out the physical features of prairies, rivers, forests, and canyons required them to stop frequently. Fuller's horse had long ago given out, so Fuller had been on foot for a while. But all three men were suffering. One of Carvalho's feet was sore from walking through the flinty mountains, clad only in thin moccasins. Fuller's toes stuck out of his moccasins, and he trudged through the snow with great difficulty. The men rested often, but at every ten steps Fuller had to stop. Finally he announced that he was giving up; he could go no farther. Carvalho was surprised by Fuller's emotional and physical collapse because he had been "the strongest and largest man in camp when the group left Westport and appeared much better able to bear the hardships of the journey than any man in it." Carvalho and Egloffstein tried to support Fuller so that he could walk, but the man's legs were immovable. Fuller insisted that the other two proceed to camp and, if possible, send him assistance. Although Carvalho and Egloffstein wanted to stay with Fuller, all three realized that they now lagged behind the main party by at least four to five miles. So Carvalho and Egloffstein wrapped Fuller in his blankets, admonished him to keep awake and stay by the trail, and then left, promising to return.

Carvalho and Egloffstein resumed their long, weary trek, following where possible the tracks of the main party. At night it was difficult to see tracks, and they had to stop often to reorient themselves. But they needed to get help for their injured comrade, and even after snow began to fall again they kept traveling. It took them ten hours to reach camp.

Carvalho and Egloffstein immediately told Colonel Frémont about Fuller, and they were shocked when Frémont said he would not send a search party to look for him. Carvalho had forgotten that the few remaining animals were needed to carry the baggage and scientific equipment of the expedition. And the driving snowstorm would make it impossible to find their trail leading back to the injured man. But when Carvalho fell weeping to the ground, overcome with sorrow and disappointment, Frémont changed his mind. He ordered Frank Dickson to take the two best animals in camp, plus some cooked horse meat, and find Fuller. The entire camp sat up all night waiting for the two men to return, but at dawn there was still no sign of either man. Frémont, who had allowed his humanity to overcome his judgment, remarked sadly that this was just what he had expected.

Now it was daylight, and Frémont decided to send three Delaware guides to find Dickson and the injured Fuller. One of them returned quickly with Dickson and the mules in tow. Bewildered by the snowstorm, Dickson had lost the trail. Although he had sunk deep into the snow, he had managed to hold on tightly to the mules. But he was badly chilled and weakened.

Snow. Of all the natural phenomena that challenged expeditions through mountains, this obstacle completely undermined the courage, both physical and mental, of travelers. Snow shut out the world, limiting vision to a small white space. Human strength gave way before the force of an endless downfall, which dulled one's sensibilities and sapped mental powers before physical strength was exhausted.

As night approached, the group spied two Delaware supporting a half-frozen Fuller, who was almost senseless from cold and lack of food. Fuller's feet were black from frostbite, which had caused his skin to decay. Even his ankles were frozen. Carvalho poured out the last drop of the alcohol he used to make daguerreotypes, mixed it with a little water, and gave it to a grateful Fuller.

This incident made Carvalho think about the situation. The men were stranded in the midst of mountains, worn down by starvation and cold, and faced with a long, uncertain distance to travel over unexplored country without enough animals to carry them. He concluded that no one would have blamed Frémont if he had refused to search for a lost and disabled man. Twenty-seven animals had already been

Trapped by snow

killed for food, and the rest were weak. No food was in sight to restore their strength, and had the event occurred six days later, not one animal would have been strong enough to carry Fuller into camp.

Carvalho knew that if Fuller had been disabled while in camp and then unable to proceed, his comrades would have had to leave him there to die alone, for "to stop, or remain an indefinite time with a disabled comrade, was certain death to the whole party, without benefiting him; his companions being so weak that they could not carry him along."[1]

The party crossed the Green River in what is now the state of Utah. Every man was weak from lack of food. And to make matters worse, everyone in the party was now on foot. There was nothing to eat, and there were no horses or mules to ride, since the animals were all carrying baggage. One of Carvalho's feet was badly frozen and painful. He had to walk slowly, and he was so far behind the others that he was always the last man on the trail. Alone, disabled, with no possibility of assistance from anyone, Carvalho felt his energy and will to live disappearing. At the top of a mountain of snow, with nothing but more snow before and behind him, he searched for smoke or some sign of the party's campsite. But he saw nothing. Faint and exhausted, he sat down on a snowbank, certain that his last hour on earth had finally arrived. With a burst of energy he reached into his pocket for the miniature daguerreotypes of his wife and children. He wanted to see them one last time. As he gazed at their faces, a miracle seemed to happen. He was reenergized, and his spirit and will to live were restored. He realized that his death would "bring heavy sorrow and grief to those who looked to [him] alone for support." Now he was determined to get to camp. His body craved sleep, a sign that he was freezing, but he fought against it. He knew that if he did sleep, he would never wake up.

Carvalho resumed his lonely journey. As nightfall approached, the cold increased and a snowstorm blew directly in his face, almost blinding him. He braced himself against the knife-sharp gusts of wind and followed the trail of the men, which had been etched into the deep snow. Finally a weary Carvalho reached camp about ten o'clock that

Painting of Sarah Carvalho, undated, by Solomon Nunes Carvalho

Joan Sturhahn Collection, The Jewish Museum of Maryland

night. Colonel Frémont was at the campfire waiting for him. As Carvalho stood by the fire warming his frozen limbs, Frémont reached out his hand and pushed on the half-frozen man's chest. Carvalho threw back his foot to keep himself from falling. When he looked up, Frémont was smiling. Any man, he said, who reacted that fast was good for many more miles of travel. Then he explained why he had "played this little joke" on Carvalho:

> *It was to prevent my telling my sufferings to the men; he saw I had a great deal to say, and that no good would result from my communicating it. He reviewed our situation, and the enervated condition of the men, our future prospects of getting into settlements, and the necessity there was for mutual encouragement, instead of vain regrets; and despondency.*[2]

During the night, Colonel Frémont pored over his maps, trying to devise a way out of their dangerous situation. When morning came, he called the men together and told them he had decided to cache, or hide, most of the baggage so the men could ride on the pack animals. The only thing the men could keep was the clothing they needed to

Two of Carvalho's children

protect them from the weather. A hole was prepared in the snow and the large buffalo-skin lodge laid in it. Then the men put in

> *all the pack saddles, bales of cloth and blankets, the traveling bags, and extra clothes of the men, daguerreotype boxes, containing besides, several valuable scientific instruments, and everything that possibly could be spared, together with the surplus gunpowder and lead.*[3]

The hole was carefully covered with snow and brush to conceal it from thieves and to mark the spot so they could recover the baggage later.

The men rejoiced that they had any animals at all to ride because by now they could barely put one foot in front of the other. Every horse or mule that died meant that a man had to walk again on his own two painfully frozen feet. No more animals would magically appear, and the men could not double up. Since there was no grass for the mules to eat, the animals needed as light a burden as possible. Indeed, when the men were able to walk, they gladly dismounted in order to relieve the mules.

When an animal was finally exhausted, one of the Delaware shot it and cut its throat. Its blood was saved in a kettle. According to Frémont's newly adopted rule, one dead animal would supply six meals for each man in the party. And any man who gobbled down his six meals in an hour or a day would have to go without food until another exhausted animal was killed. If another animal died in the meantime, an exception to the rule was made. But on no condition was a working animal to be slaughtered for food.

Carvalho observed that although most of the white men frequently went without food for twenty-four to thirty-six hours, Colonel Frémont and the Delaware always had a meal. The Indian men carefully spaced out their meals over a two- to three-day period and never ate a portion allotted for the next meal until it was time to do so. But the white men, unhappy with the size of their daily portion and miserable from cravings of hunger, secretly stole pieces of meat from the pile, therefore depriving themselves of their future allowances.

Delaware man

Western History
Collections, University
of Oklahoma Libraries

When an animal was slaughtered, the cook made food from every part of it. He shook up the entrails of the horse, boiled them in melted snow, mixed in the animal's hoofs and eyes, and produced a highly flavored soup. The soup bones were then roasted and the men gnawed on them for lunch as if they were tasty snacks. The cook burned the hair off the hide and roasted the skin until it was crisp, but when the cook offered each man an equal share of blood from the kettle, Carvalho never drank his portion. Despite his hunger, the Jewish prohibition against ingesting blood was one he always honored.

As for Frémont, he decided that he no longer wanted to eat with his men, saying that "it gave him pain and called to mind the horrible scenes which had been enacted during his last expedition." He retired to his lodge so he could not see his officers partaking of such disgusting food. Carvalho suspected that in reality Frémont ate his scanty meal alone so his men could speak freely among themselves. And the colonel was spared the complaints about his leadership and the way the men were being forced to survive.

Carvalho recalled earlier mealtimes in Frémont's lodge that now seemed like paradise. He remembered the warm fires burning in the center of the tipi and how the men sat crosslegged on soft buffalo robes, waiting for the first course to be served.

> *First came the camp kettle, with buffalo soup, thickened with meat-biscuit, our respective tin plates were filled and replenished as often as required. Then came the roast or fry, and sometimes both; the roast was served on sticks, one end of which was stuck in the ground, from it we each in rotation cut off a piece. Then the fried venison. In those days we lived well, and I always looked forward to this social gathering as the happiest and most intellectually spent hour during the day.[4]*

Although Frémont disappeared during these awful meals, when it came to hard labor, at times he joined the men. If they had difficulty finding enough firewood to burn through the night, Frémont pitched in. He helped when it took the combined efforts of six men to drag a heavy dry tree into camp for the fire.

Chapter 12

Death of a Friend

W HEN THE MEN REACHED the Sevier River crossing in Utah, they noticed numerous felled trees and dams. In a spot where the river was no more than thirty feet wide, three trees lying parallel to each other looked like a bridge across the water. The men thought they were near old Indian camping grounds. Imagine their surprise when they realized that the dams and the downed trees were the work of beavers! Carvalho could not believe it.

The men entered the Little Salt Lake Valley and moved through a pass, but they were soon encircled by mountains as they trudged through the deep snow of Circleville Canyon. Colonel Frémont was worried about finding a passage out, so he asked Captain Wolff and Solomon Everett to survey the canyon. Captain Wolff was stumped. He firmly believed that the mountain before them, measuring at least one thousand feet from base to summit, could not be crossed. But Frémont insisted. The only question was how to do it, when even the animals were slogging through four-foot snowdrifts.

Frémont, with Carvalho as his assistant, conducted the last astronomical observation in the canyon. Standing almost up to his waist in snow, Frémont worked for hours making observations and calculations with a sextant and the few astronomical tables that had not been buried. The men worked by lantern, illuminated with the last of six pieces of sperm candle Carvalho had saved from his equipment box before that too was buried. The next morning Frémont decided that, with some luck, in three days they could reach Parowan, a small Mormon settlement of one hundred families in the Little Salt Lake Valley.

Colonel Frémont led the group one thousand feet to the top of a ridge. Since the animals and the men were walking at a forty-five-degree angle, the climb was steep and difficult. Each man placed his

Carvalho and Frémont taking observations in mountains

From *Incidents of Travel and Adventure in the Far West*, copyright 1954 by the Jewish Publication Society

feet in the tracks made by the man before him. Since the snow reached up to the animals' bellies, it was of course impossible to ride them. The men stopped to rest, then forged ahead, then rested. Somehow they reached the summit. From that high point above the timberline, all Carvalho and the others could see were snowcapped mountain ranges stretching, seemingly, into eternity. He thought that crossing those mountains would be impossible.

> *For the first time, my heart failed me—not that I had lost confidence in our noble leader, but that I felt myself physically unable to overcome the difficulties which appeared before me, and Capt. Wolff himself told me that he did not think we could force a passage. We none of us had shoes.*

. . . Some of the men had raw hide strapped round their feet, while others were half covered with worn out stockings and moccasins; Colonel Fremont's moccasins were worn out, and he was no better off than any of us.[1]

Rocky Mountain peaks   Bruce Coleman, Inc.

After a short rest, Colonel Frémont began the descent. The party wound around the base of one mountain, over the side of another, through several narrow passages, and finally through what had looked like impassable canyons. Every half hour, as the group conquered one mountain after another, they noticed that the number of trees was increasing. The men had finally dropped below the timberline, leaving behind arctic cold and snowy peaks.

Early in the afternoon, the group camped in a grassy valley, and deer tracks in the snow lifted everyone's spirits. Frémont promised to award a superior rifle to the man who shot the first deer. Within several hours Weluchas had killed a fine buck and collected his handsome reward, and all the men except Fuller finally ate "a dish of wholesome food."

Fuller, who no longer could walk on his frostbitten feet, had

Black-tailed deer

Denver Museum
of Natural History

received the assistance of every man in camp. That morning, Carvalho had helped Fuller onto a mule and fixed him a breakfast of roasted prickles from some cactus leaves that he had dug out of the snow. As the group trudged down the mountain, the men voluntarily deprived themselves of a portion of their already tiny ration of horse meat so the suffering man had more to eat. But Fuller knew that neither meat nor cactus leaves could save him. He did not want to leave camp; he knew death was near.

While the men regained some strength after the meal of deer meat, a group of Ute Indians came into Frémont's camp. Their leader, Ammon, led the men out of the grassy valley and into Red Creek Canyon. There Egloffstein discovered that Fuller had died in his saddle. It is said that burial is the last thing you can do for a relative or friend. But the ground was frozen solid and the men did not have pick axes to break through it, so they could not perform this kind act for their friend. Instead, they wrapped Fuller in a blanket and laid his body beside the trail. Later, after reaching Parowan, Colonel Frémont sent back several men to perform the sad duty of burying Fuller.

Fuller's death filled the group with sorrow. He had been well liked by all the men, especially by Carvalho, who wrote,

> *No vice or evil propensity made any part of his character. His disposition was mild and amiable, and generous to a fault. Slow to take offense, yet firm and courageous as a lion, he bore his trials without a murmur, and performed his duties as assistant astronomer and engineer to the hour he was stricken down.*[2]

Chapter 13

Mormons to the Rescue

COLONEL FRÉMONT LED THE PARTY out of Red Creek, using the calculations he had made in the canyon with the help of that flickering light from the small sperm candle. And even though the trail was snow packed, Carvalho became convinced that the men had landed on a previously traveled road. He hopped off his mule and thrust his hand into the snow. To his delight, he discovered wagon wheel marks, and his intense despair turned to hope. Carvalho was starting to believe that Colonel Frémont had been "endowed with supernatural powers of vision," since he had somehow found the road to Parowan. But as often happens when one has been expecting the worst, now that Carvalho knew they were saved, he found himself

> *gradually breaking up. The nearer I approached the settlement, the less energy I had at my command; and I felt so totally incapable of continuing that I told Colonel Fremont, half an hour before we reached Parowan, that he would have to leave me there; when I was actually in the town, and surrounded with white men, women, and children, paroxysms of tears followed each other, and I fell down on the snow perfectly overcome.*[1]

Colonel Frémont and his party of starving men entered Parowan on February 8, 1854. The Mormons were expecting them, because two days earlier a man in a watchtower had reported that a group of Indians was coming into the north end of the valley, twenty miles from Parowan. The lookout and the people in Parowan had mistaken Carvalho and the other white men for Indians, since their hair was so long and their faces so dark.

Every family in the small community responded quickly and took the pitiful-looking men into their houses. They put them into warm

Col. Fremont's Railroad Exploration.

Just before getting into Parowan, one of the party, a Mr. O. Fuller, of St. Louis, died He was a brave and energetic man, and he died in his saddle. From the time the party entered the mountains until they reached Parowan, they encountered a good deal of difficulty. It was midwinter; the grass was in many places bad; the animals required a great deal of attention. Col. Fremont was determined to pursue his course, and to make all the explorations which the strength of himself and his party would permit; and game was wild and scarce. The party arrived at the Mormon settlement travel-worn and much reduced in flesh. They remained there twelve days, which sufficed to place them in excellent condition.

On the 21st of February, Col. Fremont left the hospitable people of Parowan to cross the Sierra Nevada. His course was a little south of west. The country was hilly, and in many places mountainous. About 100 miles from Parowan the party crossed the rim of the Great Basin, and reached the watershed of the Rio Virgin, which empties into the Colorado — Thence the distance to Owen's Range, which was struck on latitude 37, was about 200 miles over the same kind of country. Indeed, Col. Fremont did not know at what precise point he left the Great Basin. Here and there were fertile valleys, but the greater portion of the soil is of a rather stertile character. The mountains are composed of short irregular ranges, generally running north and south, covering nearly the whole country, and are well timbered with pine. Col. Fremont reached Owen's Mountain on the 21st of March. It was covered with snow, and presented no pass, and the party turned to the south, following the foot of the mountain about 60 miles to the end of the range. Here they saw the first human beings since leaving Parowan. These were the Horse-thief Indians, living just at the southern point of the range. They had large bands of California horses, and appearances indicated that they were constantly receiving additions to their herds from California. The whites attacked a party of them, and took 30 horses. One of the party was wounded by

"The party arrived at the Mormon settlement . . . much reduced in flesh."
(Deseret News, *June 8, 1854*)

Author's collection

rooms and clean, comfortable beds. Carvalho, who looked like a skeleton with sunken eyes and who wore clothes torn to shreds, was taken to a Mr. Heap's house. Heap cut and combed Carvalho's hair and washed his body, although he could not do much for Carvalho's frost-bitten hands, which were split open at every joint. Heap washed away the ground-in dirt that darkened Carvalho's face and hands, and Carvalho told him that the men had washed their faces with frozen snow but had no towels to wipe off the dirt. Over the next two weeks Carvalho regained his strength, thanks to the care of gentle, patient Mrs. Heap and her wonderful, wholesome food.

Although Carvalho had read about polygamy, or the practice of having more than one spouse, the Heap family was the first plural marriage he had encountered.

> *It was hinted to me that Mr. Heap had two wives; I saw two matrons in his house . . . but I could hardly realize the fact that two wives could be reconciled to live together in one house. I asked Mr. Heap if both these ladies were his wives, he told me they were . . . One mother [a third wife] was deceased, and she was also a sister. Mr. Heap had married three sisters, and there were living children from them all. I thought of that command in the Bible, "Thou shalt not take a wife's sister, to vex her." But it was no business of mine to discuss theology or morality with them—they thought it right.*[2]

In reality, relatively few families practiced plural marriage during the forty-year period in which Mormons engaged in it. Sources estimate that 10 or possibly 20 percent of Mormon families in Utah were polygamous and that few men had more than two wives. Usually only the more successful and visible leaders practiced plural marriage. In 1890 the Church of Jesus Christ of Latter-day Saints officially ended polygamy. Most plural marriages disappeared for economic reasons, such as the expense of maintaining several families, and also because of legal enactments. The United States government had passed laws making polygamy a serious crime.

After two weeks' rest, Colonel Frémont and most of the others left Parowan. They crossed the Escalante Desert from Utah to the California border at about the 37th parallel of latitude, turned southward, and crossed the Sierra Nevada south of Walker's Pass. Then the expedition made its way up through California to San Francisco. This was Frémont's fifth and last expedition, and his life as an explorer was now over. Seven of the Delaware, along with Max Stroebel, the expedition's topographer, returned to St. Louis. An eighth Delaware, John Smith, died aboard a Mississippi River steamer en route to his home.

Unfortunately, Carvalho was not yet strong enough to continue with Frémont. Fifty days of living on horse and mule meat, without salt or vegetables, had affected his digestive system and caused persistent and seemingly nonstop diarrhea. He had lost forty-four pounds, nearly a third of his normal body weight. He weighed less than one hundred pounds and was so weak that when the time arrived for him to take the three-hundred-mile trip to Salt Lake City, Carvalho had to be lifted in and out of the wagon like a baby.

Carvalho arrived in Salt Lake City on March 1, 1854. After regaining his energy, he explored the orderly city that covered four square miles. He noticed that a "delicious stream of water" flowed directly

Salt Lake City, 1853, looking south   The Church of Jesus Christ of Latter-day Saints

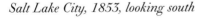

from the mountains through the center of the city and into ditches on either side of all the streets. Pure, fresh water belonged to the community as a whole, and since it was for the use of everyone, it created a "healthful influence." Gardens bloomed in front of each tidy house, and all the farmers had irrigation rights for their crops.

    Carvalho visited Territorial Governor Brigham Young, president of the Mormon Church, at the governor's residence. Brigham Young had led the first group of Mormons to the Great Salt Lake Basin in 1847. This arid, remote site was, at the time, part of Mexico. But with

Brigham Young,
date unknown

The Church of Jesus
Christ of Latter-day Saints

available water, Young and the other Mormon leaders believed that this land could look like the fertile fields and vineyards of ancient Israel. After the 1848 Treaty of Guadalupe Hidalgo was signed, Utah Territory was incorporated in 1850 into the United States.

During his ten-week stay in Salt Lake City, Carvalho and Young often took drives in Young's carriage, and Young also invited him to use his large, valuable library. It was housed in the governor's residence, a large wooden building where he lived with nineteen wives and thirty-three children. (In his lifetime Young married twenty-seven women, although not all of them were alive at the same time, and he fathered a total of fifty-six children.) While in Salt Lake City, Carvalho painted a portrait of Brigham Young and other Mormon dignitaries.

At the beginning of May, Governor Young made his annual inspection of Mormon settlements three hundred miles south of Salt Lake City. The governor invited Carvalho to accompany him to Cedar City. Carvalho, now fully recovered, was determined to travel to California using the southern route taken by Frémont in 1843 so he could illustrate the route with daguerreotypes. Carvalho had somehow reacquired photographic equipment while he was in Salt Lake City. On May 6, 1854, Carvalho found himself riding over the same route he had traveled in a wagon, as an invalid, almost three months before. Now he was part of the governor's immense cavalcade of fifty mounted men and one hundred wagons filled with men and their wives and children. Wherever they camped, Governor Young frequently invited Carvalho to join his family at their "table," a clean white cloth spread over the grass in fine weather or over a table in the wagon. The meals were large: venison, beef, coffee, eggs, and pies were served at every one.

During his annual visit, Governor Young made extensive preparations for a peace treaty with the important Ute leader Wakara (known in English as Walker) and other Utah tribes. One of the most powerful Indians in Utah Territory, as well as Ammon's brother, Wakara rose to power as a war chief of the Ute of central Utah. He was a great horseman, and he learned several Indian dialects as well as Spanish and a little English. Knowing these languages enabled him to converse and trade wisely. After the Mormon colonists occupied Ute and other Indian lands, some of them cruelly shot down the Indians. The Ute retaliated and killed Captain John W. Gunnison, leader of one of the government-sponsored expeditions. Wakara led his people in resistance in the so-called Walker War, which in actuality was a series of brief encounters in which the Indians were defeated. Although Young felt Indians were an obstacle to Mormon expansion in Utah, he preferred to coexist peacefully rather than fight them.

The Mormon cavalcade was a sight to behold. Stretching out over a mile, it proceeded to Wakara's village, situated at Chicken Creek. Wakara and fifteen other chiefs invited Governor Young and his council into the leader's lodge. Wakara even made room for Governor Young to sit beside him. At the governor's request, Carvalho attended the council. After a ceremony of shaking hands all around, Mr. Huntington, the interpreter, explained that the governor wanted to smoke "the calumet of peace" and end ill feelings between the two peoples. With the exception of Wakara, one elderly chief after another spoke about his grievances and his desire for peace or war. Everyone in the lodge smoked the pipe before the first interview ended.

The next morning Governor Young told the chiefs he wanted friendship and distributed gifts to the Indian leaders. He gave them oxen, blankets, clothing, arms, and ammunition. The council resumed and Wakara, who looked "care-worn and haggard," made his speech. Although it was cold, he wore only a deerskin hunting shirt. According to the interpreter who translated Wakara's speech for Carvalho, Wakara said that he had

heard all the talk of the good Mormon chief. Wakara no like to go to war with him. Sometimes Wakara take his men, and go far away, to sell horses. When he is absent, the Amerecats [Americans] come and kill his wife and children. Why not come and fight when Wakara is at home? Wakara is accused of killing Capt. Gunnison. Wakara did not. Wakara was three hundred miles away when the Merecat chief was slain. Merecats soldiers hunt Wakara, to kill him, but no find him. Wakara hear it; Wakara come home. Why not Merecats take Wakara?

He is not armed. Wakara heart very sore . . . Wakara no want to fight more. Wakara talk with Great Spirit; Great Spirit say—"Make peace." Wakara love Mormon chief. He is a good man. When Mormon first come to live on Wakara's land, Wakara give him welcome. He give Wakara plenty bread, and clothes to cover his wife and children. Wakara no want to fight Mormon; Mormon chief very good man; he bring plenty oxen to Wakara . . . If Indian kill white man again, Wakara make Indian howl." [3]

After the speech ended, the peace pipe was passed around and everyone at the council smoked from it. Then the council disbanded. Carvalho and the Mormons remained in their camp near Wakara's village until the next day. And during that twenty-four-hour period, Carvalho talked Wakara into sitting for his portrait. (Carvalho had been supplied with painting materials by Lieutenant Edward Beckwith, a survivor of Gunnison's expedition, who was in Salt Lake City at the time.) Today that painting of Wakara, who died on January 29, 1855, hangs in the Gilcrease Institute in Tulsa, Oklahoma.

When it was time for Carvalho to continue his journey to California, he traded Wakara his double-barreled gun and blanket for a good horse. On May 6, 1854, Carvalho set out for California with a party of twenty-three Mormon missionaries bound for the Sandwich Islands. His route to California took Carvalho through Parowan one more time. The Heaps greeted him but barely recognized his face. During Carvalho's stay in Salt Lake City, he had not only regained the forty-four pounds he had lost during the expedition but had also added an extra twenty pounds from eating the rich foods Mormon wives served at every meal. Carvalho wrote that the Heaps "could not believe I was the ugly, emaciated person whose face she washed only three months before."

On May 22 Carvalho left Utah and the journey continued across the desert. The disastrous times were at an end. He arrived in San Bernardino City, a California agricultural town of one thousand inhabitants, on June 9. His horse was lame and broken down, but the mule that carried his pack was still hearty. There had been plenty of good

Wakara, *1854, a painting by Solomon Nunes Carvalho*

The Thomas Gilcrease Institute of American History and Art

clover and grass at the last few camps. Carvalho was eager to make the forty-five-mile trip to Los Angeles, so three days later he rode his mule over "one continuous field of wild mustard, covering the whole breadth of the valley of Los Angeles." The mule traveled the distance in twelve hours.

When Carvalho arrived in Los Angeles in June 1854, about thirty Jewish people were living there without a synagogue or cemetery.

Carvalho had been away from Jewish community life since he left on the expedition with Colonel Frémont in September 1853. Now he decided to help the small Los Angeles Jewish community with some of its problems. Following a longstanding Jewish tradition of doing *mitzvah* (good deeds), Carvalho helped the group organize the Hebrew Benevolent Society, the first Jewish society in southern California. The members of this group helped one another in times of need and sickness, and they created a fund to enable less fortunate families purchase burial plots in a cemetery. On July 2, 1854, at its first meeting, the members unanimously resolved that "the thanks of this meeting be tendered to Mr. S. N. Carvalho for his valuable services in organizing this Society, and that he be elected an honorary member."[4]

Sometime after this organizing work in Los Angeles, Solomon Carvalho finally went home—although he does not reveal how—and resettled in Baltimore with his wife and children.

Chapter 14

Carvalho's Life After the Adventure

JOHN CHARLES FRÉMONT INTENDED to publish a report of his fifth expedition, and he planned to illustrate it with reproductions of Carvalho's daguerreotypes. It appears that once Frémont reached Parowan, Utah, someone went back to dig up Carvalho's daguerreotypes from their snow-covered burial site. (Wakara told Carvalho that he gave José a mule to go back to find the goods buried in the snow about one hundred miles from Parowan.)[1] Frémont's wife, Jessie Benton Frémont, reports in her introduction to her husband's memoirs that the pictures were retrieved and eventually sent by ship to the studio of the noted photographer Mathew Brady. He worked with the daguerre plates and made them into glass-plate negatives from which a more permanent form of photograph could be produced. Jessie Frémont said that

> *almost all the plates . . . were beautifully clear . . . These plates were afterward made into photographs by Brady in New York. Their long journeying by mule through storms and snows . . . and then the scorching heat tropical damp of the sea voyage back across the Isthmus left them unharmed . . .*[2]

Frémont did send the *National Intelligencer* in Washington, D.C., a brief summary of the results of his trip, which was published on June 13, 1854. He had explored some new areas and mapped more trails, but the route he advocated for a railroad was never adopted. Nevertheless, his expedition generated more support for the idea of a transcontinental railroad, which was eventually completed on May 10, 1869.

Even though Frémont never got around to writing his book, he did not want any of his men writing competing records of the expedition. Fortunately for history, two men defied his ban on the keeping of diaries. James F. Milligan kept a day-by-day journal that covered his experience with Frémont from September 6, 1853, when he joined up with the expedition, until November 25, when Frémont ordered him to stay behind at Bent's new fort. And Solomon Carvalho reconstructed a narrative of the entire expedition by combining letters he had written to his wife with the journal he had kept during the expedition. It was first published in late 1856 as a book titled *Incidents of Travel and Adventure in the Far West with Col. Fremont's Last Expedition.* The book was designed to applaud the work and accomplishments of Frémont when he was running for president.

INCIDENTS

OF

TRAVEL AND ADVENTURE

IN THE

FAR WEST;

WITH

COL. FREMONT'S LAST EXPEDITION

ACROSS THE ROCKY MOUNTAINS : INCLUDING THREE MONTHS' RESIDENCE IN
UTAH, AND A PERILOUS TRIP ACROSS THE

GREAT AMERICAN DESERT,

TO THE PACIFIC.

BY S. N. CARVALHO,

ARTIST TO THE EXPEDITION.

NEW YORK:
DERBY & JACKSON, 119 NASSAU ST.
CINCINNATI :—H. W. DERBY & CO.
1857.

Cover of Solomon Nunes Carvalho's book, 1857 edition

Carvalho wrote his narrative during the winter of 1855–56, when he got swept along in the campaign to nominate Frémont for the presidency of the United States on the ticket of the newly formed Republican Party. John Bigelow, a reporter for the New York *Evening Post* and one of Frémont's campaign managers, suggested that Carvalho take his manuscript to Derby & Jackson, the firm that had published Bigelow's biography of Frémont. Indeed, the reporter's book had included excerpts from Carvalho's diary. Derby & Jackson published Carvalho's journal as a campaign document. Carvalho needed money, so he accepted a total payment for his book of three hundred dollars rather than a royalty of five cents for every copy sold. Little did he know that before 1860 the book would go through four printings in America and would even be published in a British edition. His daguerreotypes were Frémont's property and by agreement were to first appear in Frémont's account.

It disappointed Carvalho that Frémont never published the daguerreotypes, especially since Carvalho had risked his life for them on several occasions. A great mystery surrounds the whereabouts of Carvalho's daguerreotypes, which amounted to at least three hundred in all. Historians believe that after Mathew Brady developed the plates in his studio, some were turned over to an engraver for copying and others loaned to a painter for reproduction in full color. It is possible that the daguerreotypes may have been lost in a warehouse fire, or they may still be mixed in with thousands of other unmarked photographs in some archive. Sad as it may seem, to this day no one knows with certainty what happened to them. Some scholars believe, however, that a daguerreotype of Cheyenne tipis (see page 44) at the Library of Congress may be the one surviving image from Carvalho's expedition.

When Carvalho returned East in 1854 after his long absence, he concentrated on making a living for his family, which by 1856 had grown to include one more son in addition to his two older sons and daughter. He turned to his first love and painted portraits from life or from photographs of prominent people in Baltimore or in the Jewish community. But portrait painters simply could not make a living.

Carvalho's urgent need to support his sizable family led him to investigate ways to improve the power and efficiency of the steam boiler. He invented an apparatus for superheating steam, and in 1860 the U.S. Patent Office granted him a patent. Soon Baltimore foundries, refineries, and mills were operating with Carvalho's superheater.

Carvalho channeled other creative energies into the Baltimore Jewish community. In 1857 he founded Beth Israel, a synagogue for Sephardic Jews, who followed Spanish and Portuguese religious customs. During the time congregants worshiped at this public synagogue, they heard services conducted both in Hebrew, the sacred language of Judaism, and in English. Sermons were given entirely in English. For the first time in Baltimore, the Hebrew-English prayer book of Rabbi Isaac Lesser, Carvalho's mentor and friend, was used in a public place. Plagued with financial troubles, the small Sephardic congregation disbanded in 1859. Like her husband, Sarah Carvalho was also active in Jewish community life. The year he founded Beth Israel she became president of the Baltimore Hebrew-English Sunday School. Within a year the school attracted over two hundred twenty-five students eager to have religious lessons in English.

In 1861 Carvalho moved his family to New York. He had found it too difficult to earn a sufficient income in Baltimore from portraiture and photography. In New York he painted portraits of prominent New Yorkers and even one of President Abraham Lincoln after his assassination in 1865. Carvalho based his painting, which now hangs in the Rose Art Museum at Brandeis University, on the image of the president in the April 27, 1861, issue of *Harper's Weekly*. But in 1869 Carvalho's portrait painting career abruptly ended when he developed cataracts in his eyes.

Although he was now forced to give up painting, Carvalho continued to work at his steam superheating business and invented a process for heating by hot water and steam. Perhaps months of having lived in icy-cold mountain air led him to ponder heating systems, and in 1877 and 1878 he received two more patents for his steam inventions. They had such merit that the American Institute of New York awarded Carvalho the Medal of Excellence. Thus, he found financial success as an engineer rather than as an artist.

Carvalho and his wife were active in Hand-in-Hand Congregation, a small synagogue founded in 1870 and located in New York City's Harlem. He devoted himself to writing, attempting to harmonize the Genesis account of creation with scientific thinking. But he never finished the book.

Carvalho died on May 21, 1897, at what was then the remarkably old age of eighty-two. His health had been failing since his wife's death on May 2, 1894. Both are buried in a plot belonging to Congregation Shearith Israel in New York City, a Sephardic synagogue founded in 1654 and the oldest established and continuously functioning congregation in the United States.

How fitting that Solomon Carvalho was laid to rest in the first synagogue erected in the American colonies, since he, too, could boast of several firsts: He was the first Jewish photographer in history and the first Jew appointed to be an official photographer of an exploring expedition in the American West. He was the first and only Jew to write a narrative of western American adventure in the mid-nineteenth century, and the only person to write a full account of John Charles Frémont's fifth and last expedition to the West. Carvalho's book contains a remarkable record of the tremendous personal courage and genuine perseverance it took to travel from New York City to Parowan, Utah—a distance of about 2,400 miles. By today's standards this trip still counts as a long one, even if it is made in the comfort of a four-wheel-drive vehicle traveling across the nation's superhighways. Carvalho, however, made the trip by stagecoach, steamer, pony, mule, and his own two feet in the open air. He survived grass fires, frigid winds, drenching rainstorms, driving snowstorms, frostbite, and near starvation—all the while doing the job he was hired to do—buffing, coating, and mercurating daguerreotype plates in Kansas, Colorado, and Utah.

Solomon Nunes Carvalho in old age

Joan Sturhahn Collection, The Jewish Museum of Maryland

Notes

All page references to *Incidents of Travel and Adventure in the Far West with Col. Fremont's Last Expedition* by Solomon Carvalho refer to the edition published in 1954 by the Jewish Publication Society of America.

SOLOMON NUNES CARVALHO
For more information about Solomon Nunes Carvalho, read the introductory essay by Bertram Wallace Korn in the 1954 edition of *Incidents of Travel and Adventure in the Far West* and the biography titled *Carvalho: Artist, Photographer, Adventurer, Patriot: Portrait of a Forgotten American* by his great-great-granddaughter, Joan Sturhahn.

CHAPTER 1 ~ A NATIONAL MANIA
1. Louis B. Wright, *Everyday Life in the American Frontier*, p. 155.
2. For a discussion of railroad mileage in the United States in 1849 and 1850, read Henry V. Poor's *Manual of the Railroads of the United States for 1868–69* (New York, 1868).
3. *The Plains Across: The Overland Emigrants and the Trans-Mississippi West 1840–1860* by John Unruh, Jr., pages 120 and 289, contains information about the arguments in Congress over where to build a transcontinental railroad.
4. Beaumont Newhall, *The Daguerreotype in America*, p. 88.

CHAPTER 2 ~ GETTING READY
1. Beaumont Newhall, *The Daguerreotype in America*, p. 11.
2. Robert Taft, *Artists and Photographers of the Old West: 1850–1900*, pp. 60–61.
3. Ross J. Kelbaugh in *Solomon Nunes Carvalho* (exhibition catalog), p. 33.
4. Carvalho, *Incidents of Travel and Adventure in the Far West*, p. 77.

CHAPTER 3 ~ A CAMERA, A CONTEST, AND CAMP LIFE
1. Carvalho, *Incidents of Travel*, p. 92.
2. Carvalho, *Incidents of Travel*, p. 85.
3. Carvalho, *Incidents of Travel*, p. 86.
4. Carvalho, *Incidents of Travel*, p. 90.
5. Carvalho, *Incidents of Travel*, p. 91.

CHAPTER 4 ~ BUFFALO HUNTING
1. Carvalho, *Incidents of Travel*, pp. 100–101.
2. Carvalho, *Incidents of Travel*, p. 105.
3. Mark J. Stegmaier and David H. Miller, *James F. Milligan: His Journal of Fremont's Fifth Expedition, 1853–1854*, p. 115.

4. Carvalho, *Incidents of Travel*, p. 111.
5. Carvalho, *Incidents of Travel*, pp. 115–16.

CHAPTER 5 ~ PRAIRIE FIRES AND A CHEYENNE VILLAGE
1. Carvalho, *Incidents of Travel*, p. 126.
2. Carvalho, *Incidents of Travel*, p. 128.
3. Carvalho, *Incidents of Travel*, p. 129.

CHAPTER 6 ~ SUPPLIES FOR THE JOURNEY
1. Biographies of William Bent and descriptions of Bent's fort by his son George Bent appear in *Life of George Bent: Written from His Letters*, and David Lavender, *Bent's Fort*.
2. Carvalho, *Incidents of Travel*, p. 132.

CHAPTER 7 ~ ROCKY MOUNTAIN SUMMITS
1. Carvalho, *Incidents of Travel*, pp. 143, 145.
2. Robert Taft, *Artists and Photographers of the Old West: 1850–1900*, p. 260.

CHAPTER 8 ~ HORSES AND A SURPRISE SAVE THE DAY
1. Carvalho, *Incidents of Travel*, p. 149.
2. Carvalho, *Incidents of Travel*, p. 155.
3. Carvalho, *Incidents of Travel*, pp. 161–62

CHAPTER 9 ~ TO EAT OR NOT TO EAT
1. Carvalho, *Incidents of Travel*, p. 164.
2. Carvalho, *Incidents of Travel*, p. 164.
3. Carvalho, *Incidents of Travel*, pp. 176–77.
4. Carvalho, *Incidents of Travel*, p. 177.

CHAPTER 10 ~ STUBBORN AS A MULE
1. Carvalho, *Incidents of Travel*, p. 87.
2. Carvalho, *Incidents of Travel*, p. 175.

CHAPTER 11 ~ FROZEN FEET AND DEAD ANIMALS
1. Carvalho, *Incidents of Travel*, p. 184.
2. Carvalho, *Incidents of Travel*, p. 188.
3. Carvalho, *Incidents of Travel*, p. 188.
4. Carvalho, *Incidents of Travel*, p. 198.

CHAPTER 12 ~ DEATH OF A FRIEND
1. Carvalho, *Incidents of Travel*, p. 194.
2. Carvalho, *Incidents of Travel*, p. 199.

CHAPTER 13 ~ MORMONS TO THE RESCUE
1. Carvalho, *Incidents of Travel*, p. 200.

2. Carvalho, *Incidents of Travel*, pp. 201–202.

3. Carvalho, *Incidents of Travel*, p. 259.

4. Carvalho, *Incidents of Travel*, p. 35.

CHAPTER 14 ~ CARVALHO'S LIFE AFTER THE ADVENTURE

1. Carvalho, *Incidents of Travel*, pp. 261–262.

2. Joan Sturhahn in *Solomon Nunes Carvalho* (exhibition catalog), p. 37.

Bibliography

PRIMARY SOURCES

Bent, George. *The Life of George Bent: Written from His Letters*. Edited by George E. Hyde. Norman: University of Oklahoma Press, 1968.

Carvalho, Solomon Nunes. *Incidents of Travel and Adventure in the Far West with Col. Fremont's Last Expedition*. New York: Derby & Jackson, 1857; reissued Philadelphia: Jewish Publication Society of America, 1954.

——. Letter of March 20, 1855. "Daguerreotyping on the Rocky Mountains." *The Photographic and Fine Art Journal*, vol. 8 (1855): 124–25.

Frémont, John Charles. *Memoirs of My Life, 1813–1890. Together with a Sketch of the Life of Sen. Benton by Jessie Benton Frémont*. Chicago: Belford, Clarke, 1887.

Marcy, Randolph B. *The Prairie Traveler: A Handbook for Overland Expeditions*. Washington, D.C.: U.S. War Department, 1859.

Miller, Alfred Jacob. *The West of Alfred Jacob Miller (1837)*. From the Notes and Water Colors in the Walters Art Gallery. With an Account of the Artist by Marvin C. Ross. Norman: University of Oklahoma Press, 1968.

Stegmaier, Mark J., and David H. Miller. *James F. Milligan: His Journal of Fremont's Fifth Expedition, 1853–1854*. Glendale, Calif.: Arthur H. Clark Co., 1988.

U.S. War Department. *Reports of Explorations and Surveys to Ascertain the Most Practicable and Economic Route for a Railroad from the Mississippi River to the Pacific Ocean*. 12 volumes. Washington, D.C.: U.S. Government, 1855–61.

NEWSPAPERS

"Colonel Fremont's Railroad Exploration." *Deseret News* (Salt Lake City). June 8, 1854.

Frémont, John Charles. "Big Timber on Upper Arkansas, November 26, 1853." *National Intelligencer* (Washington, D.C.). March 18, 1854, p. 3.

——. "Parawan, Iron County, Utah Territory, February 9, 1854." *National Intelligencer* (Washington, D.C.). April 12, 1854, p. 1.

——. Editorial (on general results of expedition). *National Intelligencer* (Washington, D.C.). June 14, 1854, p. 4 (reprinted as 33rd Congress, 1st Session, Senate Miscellaneous Document, 67. Washington, 1854).

"Fremont's Voyagers." *Daily Missouri Democrat* (St. Louis). June 7, 1854.

Smith, Elder J. C. L. Letter. *Deseret News* (Salt Lake City). March 16, 1854.

Transportation advertisements. *Alton Telegraph* (Illinois). September 2, 1853.

SECONDARY SOURCES

Bigelow, John. *Memoir of the Life and Public Services of John Charles Fremont*. New York: Derby & Jackson, 1856.

Billington, Ray A. "Books That Won the West: The Guidebooks of the Forty-Niners & Fifty-Niners." *American West*, vol. 4 (August 1967): 25–32, 72–75.

Brown, Ralph H. "Colorado Mountain Passes." *Colorado Magazine*, vol. 6, no. 6 (November 1929): 227–37.

Chadwick, Douglas. "The American Prairie." *National Geographic*, vol. 184, no. 4 (October 1993): 90–119.

Duncan, Dayton. *The West: An Illustrated History for Children.* Boston: Little, Brown, 1996.

Egan, Ferol. *Frémont: Explorer for a Restless Nation.* Garden City, N.Y.: Doubleday & Co., 1977.

Farney, Dennis. "The Tallgrass Prairie: Can It Be Saved?" *National Geographic*, vol. 157, no. 1 (January 1980): 36–61.

Fein, Isaac. *The Making of an American Jewish Community* (Baltimore). Philadelphia: Jewish Publication Society of America, 1971.

Fynn, A. J. "Furs and Forts of the Rocky Mountain West." *Colorado Magazine*, vol. 8, no. 4 (November 1931): 209–22, and *Colorado Magazine*, vol. 9, no. 2 (March 1932): 45–57.

Gilbert, George. "Solomon Nunes Carvalho: His Numismatic Art Circulated Among Millions of Americans Over 100 Years Ago." *The Shekel*, vol. 15, no. 3 (May–June 1982): 3–9.

Greenspan, Sophie. *Westward with Fremont: The Story of Solomon Carvalho.* Philadelphia: Jewish Publication Society of America, 1969.

Herb, Angela M. *Beyond the Mississippi: Early Westward Expansion of the United States.* New York: Lodestar Books, 1996.

"In Memoriam." *The American Hebrew*, June 4, 1897, p. 160.

Jackson, Donald, and Mary Lee Spence. *The Expeditions of John Charles Frémont.* Urbana: University of Illinois Press, 1907, 1973.

Kolatch, Alfred J. *The Jewish Book of Why.* Middle Village, N.Y.: Jonathan David Publishers, 1981.

Korn, Bertram Wallace, ed. Introductory essay to *Incidents of Travel and Adventure in the Far West with Col. Fremont's Last Expedition* by Solomon Nunes Carvalho. Philadelphia: Jewish Publication Society of America, 1954, pp. 13–52.

Lavender, David. *Bent's Fort.* Lincoln: University of Nebraska Press, 1954.

—— et al. *The American Heritage History of the Great West.* New York: American Heritage, 1965.

Macnamara, Charles. "The First Official Photographer." *The Scientific Monthly*, vol. 42 (January–June 1936): 68–74.

Marks, M. L. "The Man Who Painted Indians." In *Jews Among the Indians: Tales of Adventure and Conflict.* Chicago: Benison Books, 1992.

Mumey, Nolie. *Old Forts and Trading Posts of the West: Bent's Old Fort and Bent's New Fort on the Arkansas River*, vol. 1. Denver: Artcraft Press, 1956.

Nevins, Allan. *Frémont: Pathmarker of the West.* New York: Appleton-Century, 1939.

Newhall, Beaumont. *The Daguerreotype in America*. New York: New York Graphic Society, 1961.

Smith, Carter. *Exploring the Frontier: A Sourcebook on the American West*. Brookfield, Conn.: Millbrook Press, 1992.

Solomon Nunes Carvalho: Painter, Photographer, and Prophet in Nineteenth Century America. Exhibition catalog with five articles. Baltimore: Jewish Historical Society of Maryland, 1989.

Steinberg, Milton. *Basic Judaism*. New York: Harcourt, Brace & World, 1947.

Sturhahn, Joan (great-great-granddaughter of Solomon Nunes Carvalho). *Carvalho: Artist, Photographer, Adventurer, Patriot. Portrait of a Forgotten American*. Merrick, N.Y.: Richwood Publishing, 1976.

Taft, Robert. *Artists and Photographers of the Old West: 1850–1900*. New York: Charles Scribner's Sons, 1953.

——. *Photography and the American Scene: A Social History, 1839–1889*. New York: Macmillan, 1938.

Unruh, John, Jr. *The Plains Across: The Overland Emigrants and the Trans-Mississippi West 1840–1860*. Urbana: University of Illinois Press, 1979.

Werner, Morris Robert. *Brigham Young*. New York: Harcourt, Brace, 1925.

Williams, Jacqueline. "India Rubber Kept Them Dry." *Overland Journal*, vol. 14, no. 1 (Spring 1996): 4–8.

Wright, Louis B. *Everyday Life on the American Frontier*. New York: G. P. Putnam's Sons, 1968.

WEB SITES

http://www.jewish-history.com/WildWest/Carvalho   This site contains the entire text of *Incidents of Travel and Adventure in the Far West with Col. Fremont's Last Expedition*, unpaged and divided into thirty-eight topics. The site provides a link to the Library of Congress daguerreotype collection.

http://lcweb2.loc.gov   This site contains three of Carvalho's daguerreotypes. Enter American Memory, hit Search, and type in "Solomon Nunes Carvalho."

Index

Page numbers in *italic* type refer to illustrations.